Spiritual Wayfinding

33 Walking Meditations for Navigating Life with Embodied Wisdom

DEBORAH GREGORY

An imprint of InterVarsity Press
Downers Grove, Illinois

InterVarsity Press
P.O. Box 1400 | Downers Grove, IL 60515-1426
ivpress.com | email@ivpress.com

InterVarsity Press® is the publishing division of InterVarsity Christian Fellowship/USA®. For more information, visit intervarsity.org.

Cover design: Faceout Studio, Spencer Fuller
Interior design: Jeanna Wiggins
Cover images: Shutterstock 2478945793, Shutterstock 1960274725, Shutterstock 60233023
Interior images: Tree: The Naturalist, iStock, Getty Images Plus; Map: ilbusca, Digital Vision Vectors

ISBN 978-1-5140-1196-6 (print) | ISBN 978-1-5140-1197-3 (digital)

Printed in the United States of America ♾

Library of Congress Cataloging-in-Publication Data
A catalog record for this book is available from the Library of Congress.

33 32 31 30 29 28 27 26 | 12 11 10 9 8 7 6 5 4 3 2 1

"As a pilgrimage leader and spiritual director, I found *Spiritual Wayfinding* both practically grounding and spiritually transformative. Deborah Gregory's rare gift lies in making every practice genuinely inclusive for all abilities and neurotypes while honoring walking as one of our most essential spiritual disciplines. This is a book that will accompany me both in ministry and personal journey—each reflection bridges the practical and profound, inviting authentic encounters with God."

Tara M. Owens, executive director of Anam Cara Ministries and author of *Embracing the Body*

"In *Spiritual Wayfinding*, Deborah Gregory has managed to write a book that is a bit memoirish, creatively instructive, and oh-so-livable! This book provides thirty-three doses of pure goodness in each meditation, helping readers (literally) walk out their faith in surprising, playful, and inventive ways. I think its special appeal is for those who long to experience more of God and haven't found the traditional models helpful. I truly enjoyed *Spiritual Wayfinding* and highly recommend you read it, get on your sneakers, and practice it!"

Beth A. Booram, cofounder of Fall Creek Abbey, author, spiritual director, and retreat facilitator

"Writing this testament on the spiritual practice of walking was a hard and holy exercise and one so desperately needed in a world of chaos, static noise, and disruption everywhere. Deborah Gregory's walks, inspired by the *Spiritual Exercises of St. Ignatius*, can also significantly benefit parents of children with disabilities by encouraging walking in moments of joy, sadness, anger, disgust, and supreme fear; these exercises not only strengthen their relationship with God through prayer, meditation, and reflection but can move them toward more profound senses of purpose for themselves and their families. I appreciate how Gregory's *Spiritual Wayfinding* bridges our connection to God and to each other through touch, our senses, our voices, creativity, emotions, and the world around us."

Alexai Perez, administrative Coordinator at the Autism Society of Florida and parent of a daughter with Down syndrome and autism

"As a Jesuit who has spent many years accompanying people in discernment, I found *Spiritual Wayfinding* a deeply resonant and embodied gem. Deborah Gregory writes with the kind of contemplative attention and practical wisdom that sits at the heart of the Ignatian tradition. She helps readers listen for God in the real, messy movements of their own lives, and she does so with a light, personal touch. More than once, I caught myself nodding in recognition at her insights. This is a book I would gladly place in the hands of anyone seeking a grounded, grace-filled way forward."

Brendan McManus, spiritual director and author of *Redemption Road* and *Finding God in the Mess*

"Deborah Gregory is a wise and tender guide. In *Spiritual Wayfinding*, she helps us remember that the discernment of God's presence begins in our bodies and unfolds as we move through the world with attention and care. She leads us into an on-the-ground life rooted in creation and helps us open our eyes to the grandeur of God along the way. Life with God is relational and communal, and Deborah is writing to help us remember that we never walk alone."

Jared Patrick Boyd, pastor, founding director of the Order of the Common Life, and author of *Imaginative Prayer* and *Finding Freedom in Constraint*

"*Spiritual Wayfinding* invites you to drink deeply from God's life-giving water in your daily life! Deborah Gregory is a trusted guide and spiritual companion on a journey of spiritual respite and renewal. This book holds powerful meditations, ponderings, and spiritual practices that invite a renewal of mind, body, and spirit."

Becky Eldredge, founder of Ignatian Ministries and author of *Busy Lives & Restless Souls*, *The Inner Chapel*, and *Encounter Grace*

"*Spiritual Wayfinding* is the perfect book for your journey of faith. Deborah Gregory walks with you on the journey, sharing wisdom from Scripture and her own story of faith. With the disciples, you'll cry out, 'Were not our hearts burning while he spoke with us on the road!'"

Joe Laramie, director of Sacred Heart Jesuit Retreat

For Jim, Alina, and Maggie—

my beloved walking companions,

whose steadfast and joyful presence

inspired every step of this book.

Contents

Introduction: Finding Our Way 1

Pre-Amble: Put on Your Shoes 13

Walk 1: Right Shoe: Walk in Love. 15

Walk 2: Left Shoe: Walk with Humility 19

Part 1: Sensory Awareness 23

Walk 3: Horizon-Gazing Walk: Sight 25

Walk 4: Listening Walk: Sound 29

Walk 5: Picnic: Taste and Smell. 33

Walk 6: Forest Bathing: Touch 37

Walk 7: Breath Walking: Interoception (Internal Sensations) 41

Walk 8: Silly Walk: Proprioception and Balance 45

Part 2: Exploring Your Emotions 49

Walk 9: Awe Walking: Exploring Joy 51

Walk 10: Blueway Walking: Exploring Sadness. 55

Walk 11: Stomp Walk: Exploring Anger 59

Walk 12: Yuck Walking: Exploring Disgust 63

Walk 13: Walk Before Dawn: Exploring Surprise. 67

Walk 14: Walk in the Park: Exploring Fear 71

Part 3: Becoming Aware of Your Thoughts 75

Walk 15: Poohsticks: Releasing Sticky Thoughts. 77

Walk 16: Labyrinth Walking: Untangling Fantasy and Rumination 81

Walk 17: Creative Imagination: Making Nature Art 85

Walk 18: Collecting Memory Stones: Recollecting Grace. . . . 89

Walk 19: Getting Lost: Discovering the Prayer of Examen. . . 93

Part 4: Spiritual Orienteering 97

Walk 20: Navigating with Trees: Orienting to Divine Love. . . 99

Walk 21: Pattern Spotting: Finding Signs of God Everywhere 103

Walk 22: Tree-Eyes Trek: Pruning Attachments 107

Walk 23: Windflüchter Walk: Navigating with Wind-Shaped Trees 111

Walk 24: Desire Paths: Noticing the Way of the Heart 115

Part 5: Exercising Discernment 119

Walk 25: Bushwalking: The Courage to Want 121

Walk 26: Walking with Prayer Pebbles: Discovering What's Important 125

Walk 27: Birdwatching: Rewilding Faith 129

Walk 28: Walking Barefoot: Grounding in Hope 133

Walk 29: Labyrinth Dancing: Restorative Play 137

Part 6: The Pilgrim's Way 141

Walk 30: Rucking: What to Carry and Leave Behind 143

Walk 31: Japanese Interval Walking: Cultivating Inner Strength. 147

Walk 32: Rogation: Beating the Bounds 151

Walk 33: Walk Together: Uniting Steps, Awakening Joy 155

Acknowledgments 159

Notes. 160

Introduction

Finding Our Way

It's called wayfinding, princess. It's not just sails and knots, it's seeing where you're going in your mind. Knowing where you are by knowing where you've been.

MAUI, *MOANA*

My husband and I were navigating the fraught waters of infertility when I took an assignment to document the lives of military families during deployment. Several months into filming, a woman I followed with my video camera went into labor. I rushed to the hospital with my gear as my counterpart in Afghanistan hurried to an armored military vehicle with her gear and the pregnant woman's husband. Through the wonder of modern technology, we created a video connection between Ohio and Afghanistan so the deployed husband could "be there" for his daughter's birth.

Four weeks later, a double pink line on a paper stick indicated I was pregnant. What had happened in my body—my hormones, mind, and emotions—in that delivery room? It felt like a miracle, and I was elated! Then, terrified. Amid the joy of pregnancy, one question haunted me. *What would I do if not documentary filmmaking?* My life was nomadic. The freedom to travel around the world at a moment's notice made me feel alive. Settling down felt unsettling. But I knew in my gut that I didn't want to "be there" for my child through a video connection from wherever I was filming in the world. Something had to change.

Feeling unmoored and swept to sea, I found that none of my navigational equipment seemed to work properly. I kept asking, *Who am I? Where am I going?* I yearned for a sense of identity, purpose, and destiny. In the swell of waves, I prayed, *Lord, what should I do?*

Eventually, I felt the winds shift, and the watchperson in my heart heard a call that oriented me in a new direction. That call was to *spiritual direction*, the ancient Christian ministry of monks and mystics who served as listeners and guides to those seeking discernment and a closer walk with God.

During spiritual direction training, the aliveness I lost as a filmmaker revived through the joy of listening deeply, asking evocative questions, and discovering the sacred thread woven into each person's story. The ancient spiritual navigation techniques passed down through the Christian tradition tugged me into the harbor of a sixteenth-century theologian and Master Spiritual Wayfinder named Ignatius of Loyola, and I no longer felt adrift.

Over ten transformational months, I followed Jesus through the gospel landscape as I prayed with the *Spiritual Exercises of St. Ignatius* and took long walks through my neighborhood. Guided by traditional Christian discernment techniques, I learned to engage my senses while reading Scripture, to feel the pull of my ordered and disordered desires, and to memorize the movements of consolation and desolation mapped in my body. In this book, I will introduce you to this ancient method of spiritual wayfinding and help you explore your own embodied wisdom through walking.

WHY A WALKING GUIDE?

Ironically, this walking guide began when I could not walk. Eleven years after my vocational crisis, I faced another season of instability. Shortly after moving from Ohio to Florida, I fractured my ankle while walking on an uneven sidewalk. My life felt fractured too. I had left a flourishing ministry in Ohio and entered a period of bewildered desolation. Once again, I asked, *Who am I? Where am I going?*

During the slow healing process, I learned firsthand (or foot!) how vital embodied discernment is for navigating life's confusing pathways. Unable to practice the prayer-walking habit I had developed after my daughter's birth, I became curious about the embodied experience of walking and praying. I used my downtime to research the latest science on walking and discovered that the benefits extend from head to toe! Even a gentle stroll can improve cardiovascular health, cognitive function, and emotional well-being.

Walking also aids discernment. The physical sensations of foot compression, eye shifts, and rhythmic breathing work together to create an internal navigational system—a map of where we are—that helps the body skillfully find its way forward. I felt astounded by the wisdom God infused in our bodies. This book emerged from those long months of learning about walking and relearning how to walk. With each tender step, I found my way back to the heart of God and my life's purpose.

Walking with neurodivergence. As my ankle healed, I enjoyed pondering spiritual matters on slow, solitary walks. However, when my daughters Alina and Maggie asked to join me, these abstract reflections transformed into tangible experiences—the joy of wind-chime hunting, rescuing unnoticed snails, and spinning in the cool breeze.

My oldest daughter, Alina, is neurodivergent, a term for individuals with neurological differences, such as autism, ADHD, and dyslexia, that shape how they think, process sensory input, regulate emotions, and navigate the world. Neurodivergent people possess a unique form of embodied wisdom formed by their rich sensory experiences and diverse cognitive perspectives.

Alina's approach to embodied spiritual wayfinding during our walks captivated me. One evening, as she walked backward down the road, I asked how a neurodivergent perspective might offer spiritual insights to neurotypical folks like myself. She replied, "Neurotypical people can be pretty abstract about spirituality. They also seem to get stuck in their thoughts about God and the Bible but don't seem to have many experiences of God." She expressed a desire to find God in tangible, sensory-rich, and emotionally safe ways.

While neurodivergent individuals may experience heightened sensory and emotional processing, these sensitivities offer profound pathways for connecting with God. Alina emphasized that everyone should have the opportunity to encounter God in ways that resonate with them. "There's no shame if you can't find God in the same way others do," she said, reflecting Paul's message to the people of Athens (Acts 17:27).

This book invites you to reach out—and step forward—to find God. Although I present thirty-three ways of walking, feel free to explore the forms of embodied prayer that resonate with you. The *How to Use This Guide* section in this introduction includes a few alternatives to walking. Adapt the meditations to your needs, pay attention to your surroundings, and honor your body's strengths and limitations in your spiritual practice.

My daughter's birth was a miracle that changed my life. As I once helped her learn to walk, she is now helping me to walk again, offering a sensory-rich perspective and leading me into a spiritually enriching territory. Her embodied wisdom inspires me to explore new ways to live well in my body and to connect with God through movement. Many of these meditations feature her delightful voice, thought-provoking questions, and profound spiritual insights.

WHAT IS WAYFINDING?

Here's an exercise to get us acquainted with wayfinding:

Pause reading and turn your body to face north.

How easy was it to find north?

Did you find it with or without technology? Did you orient yourself with landmarks?

Wayfinding is the experience of embodied orientation and movement—discerning where we are, remembering where we came from, and finding our way to where we are going through the wisdom of our bodies. Wayfinding is a multisensory, emotional, and social way of navigating with mind and body integration.

Long before the development of modern navigational technology, people relied on wayfinding techniques to navigate the world and find their way home. Among the most skilled wayfinders were the Polynesian voyagers who sailed the Pacific Ocean more than three thousand years ago. Guided only by the stars, their hands, and the feel of the waves, they expertly navigated sixty-foot canoes across thousands of miles of open water and reached their destination with pinpoint accuracy.

In the book *The Wayfinders*, anthropologist and navigator Wade Davis describes how ancient knowledge was passed down from one generation to the next. Babies played in tide pools to understand the pull of the ocean. Children memorized the stars through song and mapped the movements of the sky within their bodies through dance. Without the use of a chart or compass, sea voyagers familiarized themselves with celestial movements, ocean currents, and winds until they intuitively felt them in their bodies. They measured distance by tracking the position of the stars with their hands and found their way home by feeling the changes in wave swells in their gut. The ancient wayfinder confidently navigated the vast ocean through a deep connection to the natural and supernatural forces that guide every movement.

Eventually, the ancient practice of wayfinding was lost in the riptide of technological advancements and the pull of Western cultural currents. In 1976, the Polynesian Voyaging Society set out to recover the lost practice of wayfinding by sailing the reconstructed voyaging canoe *Hōkūleʻa* from Hawaii to Tahiti, relying solely on ancient wayfinding techniques. One month later, *Hōkūleʻa* and her crew arrived at Tahiti as seventeen thousand people splashed into the waters with cheers, laughter, and dancing. The successful navigation of *Hōkūleʻa* revived a sense of identity, hope, and healing for Polynesians across the South Pacific. Wayfinding became a way of finding a current that connects the past to a vibrant sense of well-being and becoming.

Losing our way. Traditional wayfinding through an embodied connection to the stars, wind, and waves persisted until the invention of the astrolabe around the second century BCE. A precursor of the smartphone, the astrolabe functioned as a handheld model of the universe that could tell time, location, and orientation. At the center of the universe, a *you are here* pin represented the wayfinder. From this point, a wayfinder could navigate anywhere.

The astrolabe liberated navigators from needing to memorize star movements in their bodies by providing a star map they could hold in their hands. As technology advanced, human navigation skills regressed. Eventually, we lost the embodied connection to the sky and land that once guided our way. Generations removed from the astrolabe, my portable handheld navigation device—my smartphone—does most of the connecting for me. In the journal *Nature,* researchers Louisa Dahmani and Véronique Bohbot warn that relying on GPS navigation technology can reduce hippocampal brain volume, resulting in a decline in navigation skills and memory. If we don't use it, we lose it. As the Polynesian voyagers discovered, losing our sense of direction may cause us to lose our identity and way forward.

The problem is not progress but orientation. The benefits of modern navigational technology are numerous. However, the physical and spiritual postures I develop through reliance on technology move me in the opposite direction of spiritual wayfinding. Rather than looking up and around, my device draws me downward and inward. At the center of my device is me. I am at the center of the universe.

Reviving the practice of spiritual wayfinding. The vocational crisis that ended my filmmaking career was, more precisely, an identity crisis driven by questions like *Who am I? What is the purpose of my life? How do I make choices that stay true to who I am and that remain faithful to God?* Unlike the ancient wayfinders who relied on a sense of divine connection and embodied wisdom to navigate the vast oceans, I felt lost and alone. Fear and uncertainty amplified a lingering disillusionment with the world I didn't know how to navigate.

Since becoming a spiritual director, I regularly meet with pastors and laypeople who feel adrift, yearning for a renewed sense of identity, purpose, and destiny. The discernment needed extends beyond finding a career path—it encompasses every aspect of life, including our sense of identity and purpose. We need techniques to transform us from passive drifters to purposeful navigators.

Finding our way through embodied movement deeply connects our life force to God's life force in and around us. This book offers a multisensory journey that integrates mind, body, and spirit, inviting us to look up and orient our lives to something bigger than ourselves. As spiritual wayfinders, we are desperate for a fresh breath of Spirit to slip through the cracks of our everyday lives—to encounter God's actions within the flow of our own actions. We long for embodied practices that awaken our God-given imagination, emotions, desires, and embodied wisdom to navigate life with vibrancy and purpose. We have the canoe but need a revival of stargazing, dance, and attunement to the feel of the wind. *Spiritual wayfinding* invites a journey that seeks spiritual wisdom through walking.

HOW TO USE THIS GUIDE

This easy-to-use walking guidebook provides meditations to help you navigate life with embodied spiritual wisdom. Each meditation includes a short story with practical insights, walking prompts, and a Scripture passage.

The guide is divided into six parts. The pre-amble sets the pace for your journey with God, reminding you to walk in love and humility. Parts 1, 2, and 3 address the question *Where am I?*, focusing on sensory systems, emotions, and cognitive awareness. Parts 4, 5, and 6 address the question *Where am I going?* by exploring spiritual orienteering through principles of natural navigation, spiritual discernment, and transformative aspects of pilgrimage.

Although the meditations are sequential, there are four ways you can walk this book:

1. **Thru-hike:** Walk each meditation in consecutive order to integrate accruing insights into your daily walking practice.
2. **Expedition:** Use the walks on a pilgrimage, backpacking trip, sabbatical, or silent retreat. Move through the meditations at the pace of your heart.
3. **Camp out:** For those new to spiritual practices or wanting to deepen their prayer life, you may focus on specific exercises like the *Prayer of Examen* (Walk 19) or *Awe Walking* (Walk 9). Extend these meditations over days or weeks to integrate them into daily life.
4. **Field guide:** Spiritual directors, pastors, and guides can adapt these meditations as a resource for the individuals or groups they serve.

Scripture meditation with imaginative contemplation. Imaginative contemplation involves engaging Scripture with your imagination. Each meditation begins with a Scripture passage and a focus phrase to help immerse yourself in the story with your senses and emotions. You can either read the Scripture before you walk or listen to it through an audio recording while you walk.

Steps to Practice:

1. **Read:** Choose your preferred translation and read the Scripture slowly. Allow the words to wash over you without analysis.
2. **Imagine:** Read the passage again. Imagine yourself in the scene, engaging your senses and noticing your emotions.
3. **Look for God:** Reflect on how God is revealed in the passage or what God might want to show you.
4. **Carry it forward:** By placing ourselves in God's story, we can more easily find God in our own story. As you prepare to *Walk It Out*, select a word, image, or insight to carry with you.

If a Scripture passage evokes painful associations due to past misuse or abuse, feel free to meditate on the suggested focus phrase or select an alternative text that helps you connect with God.

Walk it out. Each chapter suggests a different way to walk. However, the duration, location, and way of moving are entirely up to you. Consider exploring alternate movements or accessible paths that can deepen your connection with God and cultivate embodied wisdom.

- Engage both sides of the body with activities like yoga, butterfly tapping, marching in place, or listening to binaural beats. These bilateral movements help synchronize brain hemispheres, regulate emotions, improve focus, and enhance decision-making.
- Let your eyes wander as you gaze out a window, watch scenery pass by while riding in a car, or stroll through an imaginary landscape.
- Play with a finger labyrinth, prayer beads, or a fidget toy.
- Follow a single thread of yarn or untie a knotted rope to engage the same mental and physical processes as labyrinth walking.

Explore options that work for you, trusting your body and instincts to guide you. Whatever method you choose, stay mindful that God is with you.

Rest and reflect. After your walk, take some time to reflect on your experience. Notice how you feel physically, emotionally, and mentally. Consider journaling or engaging in another form of creative expression to capture and process your insights.

Find a walking partner. A key principle in wayfinding is to *never hike alone*. Whether you physically walk these meditations by yourself or with others, finding a companion to accompany you on your spiritual journey can be beneficial. A walking partner can be a trusted friend, a walking group, a pastor, or a spiritual director who will pray with you for guidance, discuss your experiences, and help you listen for God's direction.

PRE-AMBLE

Put on Your Shoes

Begin with love and humility

toddle
lift, lean, keel, drop
steady hands catch my fall
I'm learning how to walk again
giggles
delight
knowing I am safe and loved, I
let myself fall forward
lift, lean, keel, drop
toddle

DEBORAH GREGORY, "LEARNING TO WALK"

WALK 1

Right Shoe

Walk in Love

God loves me. It still humbles me that this force that makes leaves and fleas and stars and rivers and you, loves me. Me, Maya Angelou. It's amazing. I can do anything. And do it well. Any good thing I can do it. That's why I am who I am, yes, because God loves me and I'm amazed at it.

MAYA ANGELOU, IN CONVERSATION WITH OPRAH WINFREY

---

*D*ADA WAS MY YOUNGEST daughter's favorite word as a baby. She adorably said it with a growl, imitating his deep voice. Her Dada delighted in dropping to her eye level and adoringly saying her name in response: *Maggie.* It dripped with tender affection.

Maggie learned to walk in our apartment in Israel. A few weeks before, we attempted to take a picture of her "walking on water" during a trip to the Sea of Galilee. She adamantly protested! Instead, she waited to walk in the safety of home. Her Dada offered support and helped her back on her feet after stumbles. I was ready to catch her.

Walking isn't just a motor skill. Walking is a relational skill. Babies stabilize their attachments with caregivers around the time they learn to walk. Walking strengthens these social bonds and fosters a sense of autonomy as children begin to explore. In the book

The 6 Needs of Every Child, child psychologist Jeffrey Olrick identifies *delight* as the key ingredient for developing healthy self-esteem, security, and well-being. When Maggie took those first brave steps, our family became stronger. She was seen, encouraged, comforted when she fell, and celebrated with each step. Our delight gave her the confidence to keep trying.

Recently, after fracturing my ankle, I felt frustrated that learning to walk *again* took longer than the initial weeks and months it took my daughters to learn to walk. I wondered if there was something I could learn about walking with God by learning to walk again. Perhaps *walking with God* is not meant to be a metaphor but rather an embodied experience intended to draw me closer to God.

Previously, I used the metaphor of walking with God to describe my Bible study and prayer habits, which were always stationary. I had no framework for *delighting* in God or practicing physical movements in prayer. When the storms of life shook my faith, my thoughts swirled with shame and doubt. *Is God really loving and safe? Does God see me and desire good for my life? Or is God demanding, critical, and punishing?* When I didn't perceive God as loving and safe, I viewed difficulties as punishment and sought comfort elsewhere.

I am learning that walking with God isn't just a theological skill; it's a physically active relational skill that deepens my secure divine attachment. That's why the first step in learning to walk with God is love. To "walk in love, as Christ loved us" (Eph 5:2) recognizes that love begins with God. The Evangelist John is more explicit: "We love because he first loved us" (1 Jn 4:19).

God is love. Love is the overflowing of God's very self into creation. Walking in love aligns us with God's movement of love and stabilizes us amid life's storms. God takes the first step; we respond by taking the next step.

I recently asked Alina, Maggie's older sister, about her thoughts on walking with God. "It's like when Maggie learned to walk," Alina reflected. "You will only be brave enough to take the first steps when you know you are safe and loved by God." I want to be brave like Maggie, knowing God will provide support when I falter. I want to feel my Father's eyes of delight on me, celebrating my developing skills and trusting that he will set me back on my feet when I fall.

This meditation begins a discovery journey of walking with God through embodied wisdom. Each step invites us to enter the flow of God's love and step forward in greater love in our daily lives. By walking with God, we can strengthen our divine attachment and experience God's delight. Are you ready to take the first step?

WALK IT OUT

Scripture Meditation

Read Psalm 36:5-9. Focus phrase: *God's love is steadfast.*

Walking Meditation

Before you go:

- **Hold** the shoe of your dominant foot and let it serve as a symbol of God's love. Imagine God's love enfolding you as you put on your shoe.

As you walk:

- **Chant** a phrase about God's love with each step (silently or aloud). Examples: *God's sustaining love. God is love. God loves me. You delight in me. The love of God enfolds me.*
- **Notice** how you feel in your body, mind, and emotions.
- **Delight.** How do you experience God's love and delight? What do you long for in your walk with God?

Rest and Reflect

- After your walk, reflect on this question: *Where do I need courage to step forward with greater confidence in God's love?*

WALK 2

Left Shoe

Walk with Humility

Draw me into Your healing gaze,
For I squirm before the fear of facing You, of hearing You,
Of being seen and known such as I am.

J. MICHAEL SPAROUGH, SJ, "GOD'S GENTLE GAZE OF LOVE"

AFTER MY ANKLE FRACTURE, each baby step and stumble felt humiliating as I relearned to walk. My pride kept me from accepting the support I needed. Accustomed to walking barefoot, I resisted the need to wear a good pair of shoes with ample support and stability. Frustrated by many setbacks, I gradually began to shift my perspective. Over time, I began to embrace the art of learning how to walk, not as a lesson in humiliation but as a practice of humility.

Scripture instructs us to put on humility as if it were clothing—or, in my case, shoes. Clothing tells a story about who we are: our work, our social standing, and our affiliations. When we put on humility, we wear the garments God has purposefully crafted for us—clothing that represents the dignity, love, and honor bestowed on the children of God Almighty. These specially tailored garments accommodate our unique traits, quirky characteristics, and individual limitations. They are double stitched and sturdy, designed to support the work we are called to do.

While relearning to walk, I practiced humility by wearing sturdy shoes with ankle support and a rocker sole, per doctor's orders. In contrast, pride manifests by wearing ill-fitting clothes that project or magnify a false sense of power, importance, or allure. Pride is like wearing stilettos on a hike. Stilettos do not reflect my true identity, support my goals, or honor my physical limitations. Attempting to hike in stilettos would likely demonstrate the proverb about pride going before a fall (Prov 16:18). By choosing sturdy shoes, I respect the reality of my brokenness and feel grounded as I take meaningful steps forward.

In the same way, humility frees me from wearing the ill-fitting garments of pride. It allows me to be honest about my limitations without resorting to self-deprecation, and to acknowledge my interdependence even when I feel strong. This humble awareness affirms my sense of belovedness and inspires me to walk confidently in the good works that God calls me to do (Eph 2:10). The prophet Micah summarized these good works as practicing justice, loving mercy, and walking humbly with God (Mic 6:8). More than a metaphor, the physical act of learning to walk with God illustrates the profound nature of humility. It moves me to receive rather than strive, serve rather than grasp, and love in response to being deeply loved.

Humility is a social skill I am developing with each step as I grow in my identity as God's beloved daughter. A simple practice of humility is getting dressed. Before I go for a walk, I put on my first shoe and call it *God's Love.* Divine love is the first and ongoing action. When I put on my other shoe, I call it *My Humility.* Humility is my active and embodied response to God's love. Walking humbly with God involves a continuous rhythm of God's loving action followed by my loving response as I learn to match my steps with God's.

I am learning to see myself as God sees me and to embrace the unique qualities I've been given. Like ancient wayfinding, practicing humility enables me to explore, grow, and take necessary risks as I discover my place within the grandeur of a world that is larger than myself. The more secure my connection to God, the greater my freedom, confidence, and satisfaction as I navigate life's paths.

As you put on your shoes, imaginatively clothe yourself in love and humility as an intentional way of walking with God. Be mindful of the ways God clothes you in dignity and honor. Receive God's eternal loving gaze. Each step begins with God's love, followed by your response of humility. Can you feel the cadence? *God's sustaining love. My humility. God's sustaining love. My humility.* This cooperative divine-human march is the guiding footwork of spiritual wayfinding.

WALK IT OUT

Scripture Meditation

Read Colossians 3:12-13. Focus phrase: *Wear love and humility.*

Walking Meditation

Before you go:

- **Put on** the shoe of your dominant foot and call it *God's Love.*
- **Put on** the shoe of your less dominant foot and call it *My Humility.*
- **Imagine** being clothed in love and humility.

As you walk:

- **Chant** (silently or aloud) "God's sustaining love. My humility." Imagining God's loving gaze on you, what does God see? What is true about you that you need to see today?
- **Examine** your humility. What ill-fitting clothes do you wear that magnify or project an image of power, importance, or allure? Where do you desire more self-awareness, honesty, and integrity?
- **Listen.** When you fall into a comfortable cadence, quiet your thoughts and listen for what God might reveal as you walk.

Rest and Reflect

After your walk, reflect on this question: *What humble response can I make to God's love?*

PART 1

Sensory Awareness

Glory be to God for dapple things–
For skies of couple-colour as a brinded cow;
For rose-moles all in stipple upon trout that swim;
Fresh-firecoal chestnut-falls; finches' wings;
Landscape plotted and pieced—fold, fallow, and plough;
And áll trádes, their gear and tackle and trim.

All things counter, original, spare, strange;
Whatever is fickle, freckled (who knows how?)
With swift, slow; sweet, sour; adazzle, dim;
He fathers-forth whose beauty is past change:
Praise him.

GERARD MANLEY HOPKINS, "PIED BEAUTY"

WALK 3

Horizon-Gazing Walk

Sight

The health of the eye seems to demand a horizon.
We are never tired, so long as we can see far enough.

RALPH WALDO EMERSON, *NATURE*

HAUNTED BY DISTURBING THOUGHTS, Francine Shapiro decided to take a walk. She noticed that as her eyes moved back and forth, her body calmed and the troubling thoughts faded. Curious about the connection between lateral eye movements and stress reduction, Shapiro investigated this phenomenon for her PhD in psychology. In her book *Getting Past Your Past,* Shapiro credits that happenstance walk for spurring on the development of a clinical treatment for anxiety known as Eye Movement Desensitization and Reprocessing (EMDR). In 2018, Lycia de Voogd and colleagues published a study in *The Journal of Neuroscience* confirming that lateral eye movements quiet the brain's fear signals, calm us down, and help regulate emotions as we reprocess memories.

Shapiro's lakeside walk demonstrates that our eyes do more than see the world; they also help us navigate it with embodied wisdom, emotional health, and spiritual vitality. "Eyes are responsible for mood and level of alertness" as we perceive our environment, explains neurobiologist Andrew Huberman on the *Huberman Lab Podcast*. As we admire the vivid colors of a sunset or track the swoops of chickadees, much more is happening than what meets the eye. Our eyes enhance our mood by gathering sunlight, engage balance through peripheral vision, and lower blood pressure by soaking in beautiful scenery. Optic flow—the sensation of the world passing by while walking—resets the nervous system and helps the mind let go of worries with each step. Nature-gazing walks can improve vision, promote mental health and emotional well-being, and illuminate a sense of God's presence.

I grew up believing my body's sensory experiences restricted my spiritual growth. Like Shapiro, I didn't know my eyes were connected to my physical, emotional, and spiritual health. Theologian and modern mystic Evelyn Underhill offered a different perspective in her book *Practical Mysticism*: "Our senses make us free." Our senses not only enable us to perceive the world, but they also catalyze and integrate our spiritual experiences. "The Beautiful is essentially the Spiritual making itself known sensuously, presenting itself in sensuous concrete existence," said Georg Wilhelm Friedrich Hegel in his *Lectures on the Philosophy of Religion*. Physical senses awaken spiritual senses, allowing us to experience awe as we reverence and delight in God. The sensory system invigorates nerves, emotions, rationality, memory, desire, and spirit to infuse our experiences of both beauty and pain with meaning.

An amazing hack for physical and emotional well-being is horizon gazing. Whether it's a sweeping view of the ocean or the jagged outlines of a mountain range, gazing at the horizon calms the body and soothes the spirit. Walking toward the horizon signals to the body that there's no immediate danger, just boundless possibilities stretching out ahead.

Three times a year, the Israelites set out on a horizon-gazing walk as they ascended to Jerusalem for festivals of worship. In *A Long Obedience in the Same Direction,* Eugene Peterson called their liminal journey "a time of danger, of expectation, of uncertainty, of excitement, of extraordinary aliveness."

Walking is a practice of hope. When afraid, the body instinctively freezes or runs away. Hope, on the other hand, walks forward. The journey to Jerusalem was a pilgrimage of hope. Walking reminded them of God's protection and care year by year. The horizon ignited their imaginations with hopeful possibilities not yet reached. And when they grew weary, they lifted their gaze to the mountains and sang a pilgrimage song: "I raise my eyes toward the mountains. Where will my help come from? My help comes from the Lord, the maker of heaven and earth. God won't let your foot slip" (Ps 121:1-3 CEB).

Today, walk with a grateful awareness of your eyes in three movements. First, look around. Allow your gaze to wander, and notice any shifts in mood or physical sensation. Then, look back on your life and examine the habits of the eyes that you have cultivated. How do your eye movements or watching habits affect your life? Finally, look up at the horizon as you consider Psalm 121. Reflect on where you need God's help and hope.

WALK IT OUT

Scripture Meditation

Read Psalm 121. Focus phrase: *I lift my eyes.*

Walking Meditation

Before you go:

- Choose a path in a natural setting.

As you walk:

- **Look around,** noticing your natural eye movements and what catches your eye as you walk.
- **Look back** on your life and examine the habits of your eyes. How do your eye movements and watching habits affect your life?
- **Look up** at the horizon and sky. What do you see? How does it feel to lift your head up? Recalling Psalm 121's promise that God is watching over you, what help and hope do you need?

Rest and Reflect

After your walk, reflect on this question: *What healthy habits of looking up can I cultivate?*

WALK 4

Listening Walk

Sound

All the space we cannot see is illuminated by sound.

SHEILA M. FRICK, DEVELOPER OF THERAPEUTIC LISTENING AND FOUNDER OF VITAL LINKS

MY FATHER HAD A SPECIAL WAY of calling my name. In my early twenties, I heard it for the last time on the night he died. Startled awake by the sound of my name, I sat up and listened. *Who called me?* In the quiet darkness, I wondered how it could be my father's voice, since he was lying unconscious downstairs. Fifteen minutes later, the hospice nurse shattered the silence, calling us to say our final goodbyes.

I have long marveled at the mystic quality of hearing my name pierce through the fog of sleep on the darkest night of my youth. Was it my father's or heavenly father's voice or my anxious nerves? I do not know, but I do know that it was a voice of love.

How do I hear God's voice? Many people ask me this question during spiritual direction sessions. I recently asked my daughter Alina this question during a walk. She replied, "I don't hear words. It's more of a resonance—something deeper than words. It feels loving."

There are many ways to hear God's voice. Although audible encounters are rare, some people experience God in dreams or visions.

Others find God's voice in Scripture passages that *speak* to them or thoughts that come to mind in prayer. For many, God's voice resonates in nature through sounds like thunder, wind, waterfalls, or birdsong. Many neurodivergent individuals connect to God through an embodied nonverbal sensation—or what my daughter calls *resonance*—rather than language.

When we go for listening walks, my daughter tells me she feels drawn into God's complex system, where everything works together. This awareness helps her become less self-focused and more connected to a larger context. God's voice is resonant like wind chimes and woodpeckers, inviting us to discover our place within a larger story.

Listening involves more than our ears—it engages our entire body. The vagus nerve transmits sound vibrations throughout our system, which can either calm us down or trigger a response to fight or take flight. This is why noisy environments can literally get on our nerves. How we listen significantly impacts our health, emotions, and well-being. According to a study led by Injoon Song and published in the journal *Urban Forestry & Urban Greening*, listening to natural sounds reduces stress, improves mental health, and sharpens our thinking.

However, listening is not the same thing as hearing. Hearing is the passive reception of sound, while listening actively pays attention to what is heard. Walking in nature develops our listening skills by allowing us to identify various sounds, assess their distance, and determine their direction. In a study published in *Scientific Reports*, Dr. Cassandra Gould van Praag and colleagues confirm my daughter's experience: engaging with nature encourages outward-focused attention, helping us understand our place within a broader context.

In an era of self-focus and distractions, nature calls us outward to a chorus of divine praise resonating throughout creation.

Movement also helps us listen to God. For many years, I prayed while seated, hunched over my Bible or journal, which made it hard to truly listen. When I began listening walks, my physical movement and the surrounding soundscape transformed my prayers. Prayers like *Guide me, Lord* felt more earnest when in motion.

A listening walk grounds me in the present moment. By tucking my device away or leaving it at home, I can better tune in to my surroundings and discern where I am and where I am going. An embodied listening posture deepens my awareness of God's call. I was expecting to hear his call as a roadmap for my life, but instead, I heard him call my name.

Stow away your device for this walk and allow the sounds of nature to draw your attention outward. Ground yourself in the rhythm of each step. Look toward the horizon with open hands and receive what lies ahead. Listen with the full resonance of your body. If you listen closely, you will hear the voice of love.

WALK IT OUT

Scripture Meditation

Read Psalm 19:1-6. Focus phrase: *Listen to nature speak about God.*

Walking Meditation

Before you go:

- Choose a nature-rich path. Limit the use of devices and other distractions.

As you walk:

- **Hear.** Focus on what you hear in and around you, then slowly expand awareness outward to the most distant sounds. Try to identify what you hear and where the sounds are coming from.
- **Notice** how the sounds make you feel. How does active listening engage your other senses? What memories, emotions, and thoughts are activated?
- **Listen** to nature. How does creation resound with God's greatness and love?
- **Listen** for God. How does God speak to you: through Scripture, other people, nature, a resonance, or something else?

Rest and Reflect

After your walk, reflect on this question: *What resonates with me from the Scripture passage or my experience of walking in nature?*

WALK 5

Picnic

Taste and Smell

We were given appetites, not to consume the world and forget it, but to taste its goodness and hunger to make it great.

ROBERT FARRAR CAPON, *THE SUPPER OF THE LAMB*

On pleasant days, my family enjoys taking sensory picnics. We spread containers of food—a cornucopia of flavors and textures—across a cheerful tablecloth in the great outdoors. During one picnic, my daughters pretended to be babies in ancient times trying solid food for the first time. They closed their eyes, opened their mouths, and wrinkled their noses as I slipped a spoonful of Greek yogurt into their mouths.

"Whoa, that is sour!" they exclaimed through puckered lips. "If I were a baby, I would spit that out!" The second spoon dripped with honey. Smiling, they noted a burst of sweetness after eating the sour yogurt. Finally, I spooned a mixture of yogurt with honey into their mouths. They noticed how the sweetness of honey mellowed the yogurt's sharp smell and tangy taste. They agreed that a baby would more likely eat sour yogurt if mixed with honey.

While modern curds are firm and squeaky, ancient curds were thick and creamy, like extra-pungent Greek yogurt. Fermented curds were an essential source of energy-rich dairy and gut-beneficial bacteria for children as they weaned. The prophet Isaiah foretold the messianic child would eat curds and honey when he could discern good and evil (Is 7:15). But how are curds and honey related to discernment? The answer is in the fantastic design of our sensory system.

Our senses guide healthy food choices. According to the *Handbook of Clinical Neurology*, babies naturally prefer salty and sweet foods and avoid bitter and sour ones, which might be toxic or spoiled. Distinguishing *good* sour from *bad* sour requires discernment. The first step in discernment is learning to taste and smell curds in the mother's breastmilk after she has eaten them. Tasting curds in the mother's milk indicates that the curds are a *good* sour and safe to eat. This process helps babies distinguish the good sour of curds from the bad sour of spoiled food. When the baby is ready to eat solid food, mixing curds with honey can help them accept the good sour.

In the same way, spiritual discernment is the process of savoring the good and rejecting the bad. The psalmist invites us to "taste and see that the LORD is good" (Ps 34:8) and says, "How sweet are your words to my taste, sweeter than honey to my mouth!" (Ps 119:103). Like a baby learning to discern what is good through tasting and smelling it in their mother's milk, we develop spiritual discernment by savoring the flavor of God's goodness. By learning to recognize God's goodness, we can make better choices about what is genuinely good and avoid what is not. And as we mature, spiritual discernment seeks to cultivate the sweet aroma of divine presence in our actions (2 Cor 2:15). More than making good decisions, spiritual discernment embodies the flavor of goodness in every choice.

For my family, sensory picnics are a fun way to practice the skill of distinguishing tastes, textures, and aromas. The embodied wisdom of taste and smell are gifts that guide us toward life-giving decisions and repel us from harm. Picnics include walking, which helps digestion and metabolism. In a *Livestrong* article, personal trainer Rick Rockwell recommends walking before you eat to reduce appetite, lift mood, and sharpen your mind. Walking after you eat can help control blood sugar, lower blood pressure, and improve sleep, according to a study by Tobias Engeroff and colleagues published in *Sports Medicine* journal. With a picnic, you can *feed two birds with one scone* by enjoying the benefits of walking before and after you eat.

Picnic tips: Nibble finger foods on the trail, spread fancy delicacies on cheerful linens, or eat on your patio before walking your neighborhood. Regardless of the setting, prepare foods with various textures and flavors: sweet, salty, sour, bitter, and umami. Try unusual food combinations, allowing your senses to guide your choices.

WALK IT OUT

Scripture Meditation

Read Proverbs 24:13-14. Focus phrase: *Wisdom tastes good like honey.*

Walking Meditation

Before you go:

- Choose a path with picnic tables or a suitable place to eat. Prepare a sensory-rich picnic. Bring a picnic blanket, tablecloth, plates, cups, utensils, trash bags, and wet wipes to enhance the experience.

As you walk:

- **Taste.** Notice how eating outside enhances your experience of taste and smell.
- **Decisions.** What do the situations and decisions you face taste or smell like? How might your sense of taste and smell influence your decisions?
- **Discern.** What does the goodness of God taste or smell like? How might you draw closer to God's goodness today?

Rest and Reflect

After your walk, reflect on this question: *What aroma and aftertaste do I leave in my decisions and interactions with others?*

WALK 6

Forest Bathing

Touch

As Frodo prepared to follow him, he laid his hand upon the tree beside the ladder: never before had he been so suddenly and keenly aware of the feel and texture of a tree's skin and of the life within it. He felt a delight in wood and the touch of it, neither as forester nor as carpenter; it was the delight of the living tree itself.

J. R. R. TOLKIEN, *THE LORD OF THE RINGS*

GROWING UP IN THE mountains of Japan gave me the extraordinary opportunity to practice forest bathing, or *shinrin-yoku* in Japanese. My favorite woodland spot was in a magical forest nook called Shiraito Falls. When my daughter Maggie turned nine, I had the opportunity to take my family forest bathing near my childhood home in Japan. In the idyllic woodland around Shiraito Falls, we dipped our fingers in the cool water, giggled as fuzzy caterpillars climbed our arms, and tickled each other's faces with wispy leaves. Maggie was the spitting image of me at that age. While we frolicked together under the verdant tree canopy, Maggie reached for my hand. The forest was refreshing, but my daughter's touch truly rejuvenated me.

Forest bathing is a simple practice that involves mindfully engaging your senses while immersing yourself in a natural setting. The Japanese government encourages city residents to visit places like

Shiraito Falls because interacting with nature can help lower blood pressure and stress hormones. Trees release chemicals known as phytoncides, which have antibacterial and antifungal properties. According to Professor Qing Li in the journal *Forests*, inhaling these compounds produces cancer-fighting proteins, strengthens the immune system, and lifts mood.

Contact with nature provides a touch point for connecting our deeper life to the life of God. Touch, the first sense to develop in the womb, is the most intimate sense and vital for experiencing emotions and building bonds. Unlike seeing, hearing, or smelling, touch allows us to interact intimately with the world. "You can't touch something without being touched yourself," says neurobiologist David Eagleman on his *Inner Cosmos* podcast. Through touch, we sense where we end and others begin. Touch also allows us to probe beyond our own boundaries to connect with the living essence of others. Physical senses awaken spiritual senses to connect life force to life force as we grasp God's goodness enlivening creation.

The power of touch can spark physical, emotional, and spiritual intensity. For people sensitive to touch, sensations like rough bark or prickly pine needles can be distressing. Others may crave the feel of sticky tree sap or smooth acorns. Because touch is the primary sense for integrating emotions, paying attention to *what* we feel can help regulate *how* we feel.

When Jesus healed people, he often did so through touch. I asked my touch-sensitive daughter why Jesus chose to touch those he healed. She replied, "Perhaps he wanted to touch their hearts." Forest bathing is more than tree hugging, although I highly recommend hugging a tree. Forest bathing is an opportunity to let God touch your heart. God's loving touch is like a master gardener tending to needs, binding wounds, healing rot, and pruning what is dead so we can flourish (Jn 15). The gardener's touch rejuvenates our life.

Plunge yourself in the life of the forest, growing aware of God's abiding life as you walk. Under the lush canopy of trees, remember that you are God's child, made in his image and created to flourish. Inhale a deep breath, expressing gratitude for the healing phytoncides that trees release. Walk slowly, engaging all your senses as you embrace the joy of nature. Notice how trees nourish the life around them.

After a while, find a tree that draws your attention. Spend five minutes getting in touch with it—place your hands on the bark and observe texture, temperature, and movement. How does the tree make you feel? Can you sense the essence of life and the urgency toward flourishing? Comparing your life to a tree, where might God be cultivating fruit or pruning away dead branches? Allow God to touch your heart and rejuvenate your life.

WALK IT OUT

Scripture Meditation

Read Psalm 1. Focus phrase: *Delight in the Lord like a tree beside water.*

Walking Meditation

Before you go:

- Choose a path among trees or plant life.

As you walk:

- **Breathe** in the phytoncides and offer gratitude.
- **Go slowly** and engage your senses. What does nature reveal about God's life?
- **Touch life.** Spend five minutes touching a tree or plant, noticing its temperature, texture, and movements. How does the feel of the tree make you feel?
- **Be touched.** Reflecting on Psalm 1, compare your life to a tree. What does it reveal to you about your life? Ask God to touch your heart with delight and flourishing.

Rest and Reflect

After your walk, reflect on this question: *Where is God cultivating fruit or pruning dead branches in my life?*

WALK 7

Breath Walking

Interoception (Internal Sensations)

When we focus on the breath, we are focusing on the life force. Life begins with our first breath and will end after our last. To contemplate breathing is to contemplate life itself.

LARRY ROSENBERG, *BREATH BY BREATH*

ONE, TWO, THREE, FOUR. French economist Édouard Stiegler counted four steps to each foggy exhale sparkling in the cool springtime air as Kuchi camel drivers approached. As an avid walker, Stiegler marveled at the Kuchis' ability to walk hundreds of miles in just a few days. Although Stiegler had come to Afghanistan on an economic mission, his interactions with the nomadic wayfinders inspired him to study rejuvenating breathing techniques for long-distance walkers.

In the cool weather, Stiegler watched a fascinating breathing pattern materializing with each frosty breath. The camel drivers took four steps with each inhale and four steps with each exhale. His exploration culminated in the publication of *Regeneration Through Afghan Walking*, a book that gained popularity among European walkers and intrigued the global medical community.

According to Stiegler, the secret of *Afghan Walking* is the synchronization of breath and step. Using a breath-to-apnea ratio of 3:1, walkers inhale for three steps, rest their breath on the fourth step, and then exhale for three steps, resting on the fourth. This oxygen-rich form of walking improves circulation, stabilizes heart rate, and strengthens muscles, making it a favorite among long-distance walkers and pilgrims for building stamina. "Walking with breathing also improved patients' anxiety and quality of life," state researchers Chiao-Hsin Teng and colleagues in the *European Journal of Cardiovascular Nursing.*

The approach is simple. However, mastering the technique requires focused body awareness called *interoception.* While we rely on our five external senses—hearing, sight, touch, taste, and smell—to interact with the world, interoception engages awareness of our internal state, including sensations like hunger, fatigue, tension, or breath. Often called the *sixth sense,* interoception guides emotions and decision-making, which explains why skipping meals can lead to feeling *hangry.* Because we think and feel with our bodies, focused breathing is a powerful interoceptive exercise for regulating emotions, reducing anxiety, and enhancing overall well-being.

Scripture associates breath with the life of God. The Hebrew word *ruach* and the Greek word *pneuma* mean breath, referring to the flow of air that fills our lungs. They also both mean *spirit,* representing the flow of life that animates our being. In Genesis, God's breath animated the human form, highlighting the sacredness of breath. Job affirmed this by stating, "The Spirit of God has made me, and the breath of the Almighty gives me life" (Job 33:4).

Early Christians practiced breath prayer to acknowledge divine life as the source of human life and deepen awareness of God's life abiding within the human body. There are many ways to pray with breath. A simple technique is to focus on your breath and become mindful of God's presence with and in you. Choose a word like *maranatha* (meaning "Come, Lord Jesus"), to pray with each exhale. I often pray using a phrase: inhaling with *I receive your life, O God,* and exhaling, *I release everything to your care.*

Regardless of the chosen words, synchronizing our breath, steps, and prayers can awaken us to God's abiding presence. To walk with the Spirit is to be alive, in motion, and animated by God's life. Breath prayer grounds us in the present moment, rejuvenating God's life in us and our life in God with every step.

Begin your walk with an interoception check-in through a meditative body scan. Start by wiggling your toes and directing your attention to your feet. Gradually move your focus up to your head, observing any tension, pain, temperature changes, hunger, or other sensations in your body. End the scan with three deep breaths. Carry this interoceptive awareness with you during your walk. Allow the invigorating practice of synchronizing movement and breath to help you stay attentive to the present journey rather than the destination. Let each breath and step rejuvenate God's life in you and your life in God.

Tips for breath walking: Select a level path to maintain a smooth rhythm between breath and steps. Be patient; synchronizing these movements takes time. Allow your breath to be a prayer. Once you feel comfortable with breath walking, try adding a prayer word or phrase.

WALK IT OUT

Scripture Meditation

Read Acts 17:24-28. Focus phrase: *In God I live and move and have my being.*

Walking Meditation

Before you go:

- Choose a level path.
- Begin with a body scan.

As you walk:

- **Breathe**. Begin by taking three deep, interoceptive breaths as you pray: *I receive your life, O Lord (inhale); I release everything to your care (exhale).*
- **Walk** at a comfortable pace and breathe naturally. Notice your internal state.
- **Synchronize** breath and step as you inhale for three steps, pause breath for one step, exhale for three steps, and pause breath for one step. Repeat this 3:1 ratio (inhale 1-2-3-x; exhale 1-2-3-x).
- **Breath Prayer.** Becoming aware of God's animating life in you and around you, add a prayer word or phrase with each exhale.

Rest and Reflect

After your walk, reflect on this question: *How does breath walking deepen my sense of God's animating life?*

WALK 8

Silly Walk

Proprioception and Balance

"Let the wild rumpus start!"

MAURICE SENDAK, *WHERE THE WILD THINGS ARE*

Mom, let's take a walk where we feel our bodies in motion!" my eleven-year-old daughter, Alina, exclaimed as she lifted her leg and took a big, wobbly step. We skipped in circles, sauntered backward, and grapevine shuffle-jogged sideways. Each silly step brought smiles and laughter as we walked catawampus through the neighborhood.

In the 1970s, Monty Python coined the term *Silly Walk* with their satirical comedy sketch titled "Ministry of Silly Walks," in which Mr. Teabag oversees development grants for silly walking. In this skit, Mr. Teabag demonstrates the humorous inefficiency of silly walking with exaggerated strides and high kicks, poking fun at the British government's inefficiency. Surprisingly, researchers discovered that the inefficiency of Silly Walking can be quite beneficial.

Professor Glenn Gaesser from Arizona State University discovered that Mr. Teabag's Silly Walk uses two and a half times more energy than walking normally. Just eleven minutes of daily Silly Walking can provide the same intensity as seventy-five minutes of vigorous weekly exercise. Not only does silly walking benefit health, but it also induces laughter and improves mood. Gaesser told *Talker News* that he hoped the research would "empower people to move their own bodies in more energetic—and hopefully joyful—ways."

In a world obsessed with efficiency, unconventional walking may seem absurd. However, silly movements engage the often-overlooked proprioception (sense of movement) and vestibular (sense of balance) sensory systems, which are crucial for managing sensory experiences and regulating emotions. In the book *Proprioception*, researchers Alejandra Vasquez-Rosati and Carmen Cordero-Homad advocate for proprioceptive activities like jumping and twirling to foster calmness and evoke positive emotions like happiness and joy. As Tony Robbins states in *Awaken the Giant Within*, "Emotion is created by motion."

When King David brought the ark of the covenant to Jerusalem, he led a parade of worshippers who danced with all their hearts before the Lord (2 Sam 6). David's wife mocked him for leaping and whirling, viewing it as inappropriate behavior for a king. Yet, David could cast aside his inhibitions and disregard her opinions by focusing his delight on God. As he danced with all his might, his proprioceptive receptors connected his movements with the joy of worship.

While Silly Walking through our neighborhood, I asked Alina if she ever felt afraid of appearing foolish. She replied, "I think we all have inhibitions, but we just don't realize what holds us back." Confronting our inhibitions is the first wobbly step of Silly Walking. Many factors can restrict our sense of freedom, but the fear of others' perceptions can lead us to walk through life with anxious rigidity. Each of us has an audience—someone or a group whose opinions matter most to us. We might seek peer acceptance, parental approval, or recognition from those in power. For many Christians, fearing God's judgment can cause them to walk through life as if on a tightrope. Often, we don't realize how the opinions of others influence our actions until we face the sting of ridicule. David's story invites us to follow and worship God freely and joyfully.

While Silly Walking has many benefits, it also comes with risks like tripping, falling, being teased, or stepping out of line. However, a sense of freedom emerges when we are willing to take risks, do something unexpected, and dance with abandon. These silly movements can help us engage our proprioception and shake off our perceptions of others' opinions as we walk with God.

You don't need a development grant from the Ministry of Silly Walks to create your own Silly Walk. Simply grant yourself permission to let loose and see what silliness emerges. Try joyful movements like jumping, leaping, whirling, and spreading your arms. Alternatively, focus on your body's sensations through slow and gentle silliness. Choose movements that suit your abilities and limitations.

You can Silly Walk anywhere! Don't be afraid to laugh at yourself or be laughed at—embrace joy and resist shame. Just ensure your Silly Walk is your own—never mimic or mock the movements of others. As you engage in the playful movement, consider how you can loosen up, resist the pressures of efficiency, step out of your comfort zone, and experience the joy of the Lord as your strength.

WALK IT OUT

Scripture Meditation

Read 2 Samuel 6:14-23. Focus phrase: *Dance before the Lord with all your might.*

Walking Meditation

Before you go:

- Choose a level walking path that is free of obstructions. Consider walking with a companion and delighting in each other's silliness.

As you walk:

- **Feel your body** in motion. What do you notice? Observe how often you smile or giggle during your walk.
- **Notice your emotions.** What do you feel? How concerned are you with what others think?
- **Loosen up.** Where do you desire more freedom? Is there something silly you've avoided for fear of ridicule? What hinders the free-flowing joy of God's presence?

Rest and Reflect

After your walk, reflect on this question: *How can I step out of my comfort zone to experience more freedom in life and in my relationship with God?*

PART 2

Exploring Your Emotions

Nothing is more practical than
finding God, i.e., than falling in love
in a quite absolute, final way.
What you are in love with,
what seizes your imagination, will affect everything.
It will decide what will get you out of bed in the morning,
what you do with your evenings, how much you drink,
how you spend your weekends and summers,
with what depth and fullness you give yourself
in obedience and availability, what you read,
who you know, what makes you angry,
what breaks your heart, and what amazes
you with joy and gratitude.
Fall in love, stay in love—
and it will decide everything.

JOSEPH WHELAN, SJ[1]

WALK 9

Awe Walking

Exploring Joy

All this he saw, for one moment breathless and intense, vivid on the morning sky; and still, as he looked, he lived; and still, as he lived, he wondered.

KENNETH GRAHAME, *THE WIND IN THE WILLOWS*

MY FIRST TREK INTO Red Rocks Park in Colorado was awesome. The Rocky Mountains are majestic from a distance, but as my friend and I drove closer, goosebumps erupted down my arms. I felt small and vulnerable in the shadows of the massive mountains. In the park, my initial shock turned into wonder as I wandered among the giant sandstone formations glowing in vibrant red and orange hues in the late afternoon sun.

The sun had set by the time we reached the iconic Red Rocks Amphitheatre, a vast 10,000-seat open-air auditorium. Nestled between two colossal monoliths, Ship Rock and Creation Rock, the natural acoustics and sensory richness of Red Rocks Amphitheatre are famous for their mystical, otherworldly quality. To our surprise, we stumbled into a free performance by the Denver Symphony Orchestra. Climbing to the back of the amphitheater, I gasped at the breathtaking sight of the Denver skyline engulfed in a storm. Lightning danced across the night sky as the strings trembled and the timpani rolled. Heaven and earth intertwined with astonishing wonder. Awestruck, I could only pray one word: *Wow!*

In the book *Awe: The New Science of Everyday Wonder and How It Can Transform Your Life,* researcher Dacher Keltner defines awe as "being in the presence of something vast and mysterious that transcends your current understanding of the world." It connects our small selves to a larger reality. But when awe awakens joy, the transcendent otherness of awe intertwines with the intimacy and presence of joy. This paradoxical union makes us feel alive and meaningfully entangled with the beautiful vastness beyond ourselves.

Awe is a social emotion that connects us with something larger than ourselves, making us less competitive and more generous. In *Greater Good Magazine,* Keltner states that without awe, we are more "individualistic, more narcissistic, more materialistic, and less connected to others." However, experiencing awe with others through song, story, and ritual can even synchronize brain patterns, hormone levels, and heart rates to deepen our sense of connectedness, cooperation, and purpose. When awe intertwines with joy, we feel motivated to seek the good, find meaning, and celebrate life's connections.

Joy-infused awe awakens a spiritually transformative state that Saint Ignatius referred to as *affectionate awe* in his *Spiritual Diary.* This paradoxical experience allows us to feel the mingling of God's intimate presence and mysterious otherness. Affectionate awe works differently than fear. "Awe, unlike fear, does not make us shrink from the awe-inspiring object, but, on the contrary, draws us near to it," writes Rabbi Heschel in *God in Search of Man.* "This is why awe is compatible with both love and joy." Affectionate awe became central to Ignatius's practice of spiritual discernment, compelling him to greater love, the greater glory of God, and the greater good. It ignited a vision of *contemplation in action* that catalyzed an apostolic movement of justice, healing, education, and scientific innovation that spread throughout the world.

For spiritual wayfinders, affectionate awe expands our vision of God's kingdom. Just as a symphony follows the conductor's movements, affectionate awe attunes us to the movements of the divine conductor and inspires us to play our part. In a breathtaking dance, heaven and earth intertwine as each note yields and flows in a dynamic interplay of layers, textures, and rhythms. Awe calls the small self to surrender to the great mystery. It bids us to unite with God to create a more beautiful world.

You don't need to visit the grandeur of Red Rocks to experience awe. Awe can be awakened anywhere by paying attention to the small wonders around us. In a 2020 *Emotion* article titled "Big Smile, Small Self," researchers Virginia Sturm and colleagues advocate for fifteen minutes of daily awe-walking to boost joy and meaningful connection to others. There's no set formula for awe-walking—simply walk with wonder. Lean in with curiosity and punctuate prayers with *Wow!* Look for signs of connectivity and cooperation. Seek out intriguing sights—a labyrinth of roots, an intricate spider's web, or the glimmer of the International Space Station streaking across the evening sky. Listen for the sounds of God's symphony calling you to participate in something awesome.

WALK IT OUT

Scripture Meditation

Read Luke 2:8-20. Focus phrase: *Awed shepherds join the movement.*

Walking Meditation

Before you go:

- Choose a path suitable for wandering and exploring.
- Consider listening to Beethoven's *Symphony No. 9 (Ode to Joy)* or another meaningful piece of orchestral music before or during your walk.

As you walk:

- **Awe.** Follow curiosity and engage your senses to notice patterns, symmetry, and beauty. Notice feelings of small self, vastness, and wonder.
- **Connection.** Look for signs of connection and cooperation as you consider your context within the ecosystem and your role within God's kingdom.
- **Joy.** When joy surfaces, notice how it feels in your body. How does awe inspire joyful connection with something bigger?

Rest and Reflect

After your walk, reflect on this question: *What part does awe inspire me to play in God's great symphony?*

WALK 10

Blueway Walking

Exploring Sadness

The water understands.

RALPH WALDO EMERSON, *WATER*

SAINT IGNATIUS OF LOYOLA understood the emotional highs and lows of the spiritual journey. Following the exhilarating joy of conversion, he sank into deep despair. After weeks of extreme fasting, he was found unconscious and taken to a convent where wise spiritual counselors helped him regain physical, mental, and spiritual health.

While recovering, Ignatius found solace on the banks of the Cardoner River. Watching the deep water flow, he reflected on the currents of his own life. Sadness is fluid like water. It tends to find the path of least resistance, reroutes to bypass difficulty, and swirls inward into eddies when the way forward is blocked. As Ignatius examined his emotions, he began to see how their flow directed the course of his life.

Rather than viewing sadness as a bad emotion, Ignatius saw it as a natural but difficult emotion. Everyone goes through periods of emotional sadness in response to loss, change, and hardship. However, longer-lasting intense states like depression and despair often require help from knowledgeable counselors and doctors. Ignatius experienced a third state he called *spiritual sadness.* When sadness drifted him away from the love of God toward distractions, fear, or false comforts, he called it *desolation.* He realized that even good religious practices, like fasting, had pulled him away from God's life and love. With the help of wise counsel, he developed healthier prayer practices that redirected the flow of his life back toward divine love.

Not all sadness is spiritual sadness. Sometimes, we experience God's consolation alongside grief, while other times, spiritual sadness arises amid times of ease. Often, spiritual sadness coincides with sorrow and depression. Seeking help from counselors and doctors is essential, as spiritual sadness often flows with states of emotional and mental sadness.

How can we tell if our sadness is spiritual sadness? In his fourth rule of discernment, Ignatius advised his wayfinding companions to recognize spiritual sadness through signs like feeling spiritually tepid, apathetic, lazy, or dark. Notice when you feel easily agitated, drawn to base things, or struggle with temptation. Pay close attention to diminishing confidence, hope, love, or sense of God's nearness.

Spiritual sadness is not a sin. It is a normal but difficult state in which we have lost connection to the current of love. Instead of avoiding or fixing the sadness, the invitation is to reconnect with love. God calls us to come, weep, and pray when we're sad—to walk beside the waters of grief and trust the everlasting current of love (Jer 31:1-9).

Divine encounters can happen anywhere, but there is something special about meeting God near water. Blueways—routes along waterways like rivers, coastlines, lakes, or canals—naturally soothe and inspire awe. The sensory-rich sounds, sights, and smells of waterways can wash away stress, expand mental openness, and deepen a peaceful state known as *blue mind.* According to Catherine Kelly, author of *Blue Spaces: How and Why Water Can Make You Feel Better,* walking along blueways can significantly enhance mental well-being. When we feel stagnant, flowing water reminds us that life keeps moving with endurance, possibility, and renewal. In the words of Winnie the Pooh in A. A. Milne's *The House at Pooh Corner*, "Rivers know this: there is no hurry. We shall get there some day."

Water is a precious resource that is diminishing in many areas worldwide. Begin this meditation by expressing gratitude for the water that sustains you. Find a walking path where you can observe the movements or sounds of water. If you cannot access natural waterways, look for a fountain, reflecting pool, or any water feature, commonly found at university campuses, hotels, and museums. Alternatively, you can use an app that offers meditative water sounds. As you observe the movements of water, reflect on your own emotional state. Notice what difficult emotions arise and how they move you toward or away from God's love. Consider what steps you can take to reconnect with that ever-flowing current of love.

WALK IT OUT

Scripture Meditation

Read Jeremiah 31:8-9. Focus phrase: *God leads me beside streams of water.*

Walking Meditation

Before you go:

- Choose a path near water. Express gratitude for the sustenance of water.

As you walk:

- **Sense.** Engage your senses as you walk near water. What does water reveal about the flow of your life?
- **Notice.** Bring to mind something that stirs sadness, noticing how your body feels.
- **Feel** how sadness affects your body, mind, and mood. Does sadness move you toward or away from God's life and love? Seek help where needed.
- **Meditate** on God's words to Jeremiah: *I have loved you with an everlasting love; I have drawn you with an unfailing kindness. I will build you up again.* Allow God's everlasting love to wash over you.

Rest and Reflect

After your walk, reflect on this question: *What movements of spiritual sadness can I redirect toward love?*

WALK 11

Stomp Walk

Exploring Anger

Anger is a catalyst. Holding on to it will make us exhausted and sick. Internalizing anger will take away our joy and spirit; externalizing anger will make us less effective in our attempts to create change and forge connection. It's an emotion that we need to transform into something life-giving: courage, love, change, compassion, and justice.

BRENÉ BROWN, *BRAVING THE WILDERNESS*

IGNATIUS, A KNIGHT-TURNED-WAYFINDER, was stomping mad but could not stomp his foot. Ten months earlier, a cannonball had shattered his leg during a battle he insisted on fighting. As a sixteenth-century knight, his quest for power and prestige in court life had also shattered. During the long months of recovery, he experienced a dramatic conversion and a desire for pilgrimage. As soon as he could mount a saddle, Ignatius embarked on a quest to transform the hot-tempered warrior into a contemplative pilgrim.

Early in the journey, Ignatius burned with murderous rage toward a man who mocked his faith. As the man galloped away, the warrior in Ignatius wanted to challenge him to a duel. But the pilgrim in Ignatius questioned whether his rage stemmed from true love for God or from wounded pride. Torn about what to do,

Ignatius released the reins of his horse. If the horse continued toward town, he would fight; if it turned toward the mountains, he would move on. Providentially, the horse veered toward the mountains.

Brad Bushman, a researcher at The Ohio State University who studies anger, notes that most people (including Ignatius) believe there are only two options for handling anger: vent or suppress it. Both methods are harmful to our health, but venting is worse because it conditions us for aggression. In an article for *Clinical Psychology Review*, Bushman suggests a more constructive third option: Turn down the heat and channel angry energy into something positive.

Anger is not inherently negative or sinful; it is a God-given emotion intended to ignite loving action. It's easier to react in anger than to act in love. That's why it's essential to calm the body and regulate emotions before taking action. Ignatius *turned down the heat* by releasing the reigns and allowing the rhythmic trotting and bumpy saddle to engage his proprioceptive system. Physical activities like nature walks and focused breathing are other simple but powerful ways to reduce anger's intensity. So is saying a prayer. "We found that prayer really can help people cope with their anger," Bushman told *Ohio State News*.

Spiritual wayfinding explores the impulses and habits we have developed in expressing or suppressing anger. We prayerfully ask: *Where is this anger leading me?* Does it draw me closer to God and empower love, justice, and mercy? Or is it fueled by fear, pride, or frustration because I'm not getting what I want? When anger repels us from love, Ignatius offers a paradoxical strategy in his *Spiritual Exercises*: do the opposite. If you feel like lashing out, respond gently. Or if you tend to suppress anger, instead express how you feel and what you need.

While it may feel uncomfortable to act against our unhealthy impulses when angry, engaging in opposing behaviors can break old habits and energize loving actions. First Corinthians 13 illustrates how love resolves to transform anger: when anger is irritable, love is patient. When anger is rude, love is kind. When anger boasts, love praises others. When anger insists on its own way, love defers to others. When anger harms, love protects.

Consider how you can transform angry habits into loving actions. Using 1 Corinthians 13 as a guide, pair a love resolution with a paradoxical stomp, like stomp dancing, stomping like a gentle giant, or puddle stomping, to channel anger into positive action. Stomp walking a love resolution can be a powerful—and playful—way to transform anger into positive action. This proprioceptive movement calms the body, regulates emotions, and reinforces your commitment to love. Chant your resolution with each stomp, letting the weight of anger strengthen your resolve to love and nurture the holy flame of God's life and love within you.

Stomp-walking tips: If anger arises, slow down to let your body calm. Reflect on what sparks your anger and the emotions beneath them. Resolve to act in ways that reflect God's justice and love.

WALK IT OUT

Scripture Meditation

Read 1 Corinthians 13:1-8. Focus phrase: *Love transforms anger.*

Walking Meditation

Before you go:

- Choose a nature path.
- Create a *love resolution*: When anger _______, love __________.

As you walk:

- **Resolve.** Reflect on something that ignites anger and how it moves you toward or away from love. Hold your anger in the light of God's justice, mercy, and love as you declare your *love resolution.*
- **Feel** how anger affects your body, mind, and emotions.
- **Stomp.** Choose a stomp that complements your *love resolution.* Identify old habits you want to change and new habits you can practice to fuel love.
- **Chant** your *love resolution* with each stomp, using the energy of your anger to strengthen your resolve to love.

Rest and Reflect

After your walk, reflect on this question: *How can I channel my anger into loving action today?*

WALK 12

Yuck Walking

Exploring Disgust

He is ready to enter into the muck with us . . . as a place where holiness happens: where sludge becomes sacramental, and through grimy eyes we begin to behold the face of Love, beholding us right back.

JAN RICHARDSON, MEDITATION ON *MYSTERIES OF THE MUD*

WHEN MY DAUGHTER SUGGESTED taking a *Yuck Walk*, I wrinkled my nose and raised an eyebrow. Disgust is a strong emotion I try to avoid, but her invitation piqued my curiosity enough to ask what she meant by a Yuck Walk. She explained that we would examine our feelings—both emotional and physical—while poking, smelling, hearing, and inspecting gross things we would encounter along a neighborhood walk. We agreed not to touch anything toxic like animal poop, cigarette butts, or dead things. To intensify our experience, we decided to walk barefoot, remembering that Jesus willingly meets us in the muck without fear of contamination.

Disgust is an important emotion that highlights our values and establishes boundaries as we navigate the world. Operating on binary logic, disgust differentiates purity from impurity. This distinction protects fragile and vulnerable things like food and medicine from stronger external contaminants. However, disgust can't always be trusted. It unconsciously influences our judgment and arouses irrational thoughts and sensory experiences that are often hard to recognize or control. When we feel disgust, the invitation is to examine it rather than avoid it.

While examining disgust on our Yuck Walk, my daughter and I noticed surprising similarities between disgust and empathy. Both emotions manifest physically with furrowed brows, narrowed eyes, and pursed lips. Socially, both disgust and empathy help define the boundaries between ourselves and others and influence how we interact with one another.

Highly empathetic people are often more sensitive to disgust, which can motivate them to advocate for causes such as environmental conservation and social justice. However, when we respond to feelings of disgust without empathy, it can result in cruel and dehumanizing actions that harm others, create divisions, or impose moral or social control. Disgust is an essential emotion that helps protect us from pathogens and diseases. The binary logic of disgust alerts us when fragile physical items are tainted by stronger external contaminants. However, Seattle School of Theology and Psychology professor Paul Hoard and practical theologian Billie Hoard caution against using this binary logic to promote social or moral stigmatization. In a *Journal of Psychology and Theology* article, they explore the theological and psychological implications of disgust, arguing that sin is not stronger than holiness. Instead, the gospel asserts that "the impure is made pure through contact with the Divine." God is the potent, contaminating, boundary-crossing agent who transforms, purifies, and makes holy.

God embraces what we deem disgusting. God became flesh through the experience of childbirth in a dirty stable and amid oozing bodily fluids. Jesus practiced ministry methods that seemed disgusting, like mixing saliva and mud to heal, washing stinky feet, touching festering wounds, and probing ear canals with his finger.

Even Communion draws on cannibalistic language that may disgust us as it invites eating bread and wine as the body and blood of Christ.

Astonishingly, the Eucharist flips the logic of disgust upside down by embodying the ultimate form of *eucontamination*—contamination for good. God is not contaminated; God is the good "contaminant" who contagiously cleanses, purifies, and heals what is unclean, impure, and broken. In their article, Paul and Billy Hoard highlight God's *eucontaminating* love as a "corrective lens through which the church can reimagine its role in the world."

While Yuck Walking, I asked my daughter what to do if we felt disgusted. She wisely answered, "Perhaps the best antidote to disgust is to care." Instead of allowing disgust to breed hostility and dehumanizing attitudes like racism, sexism, and ablism, God calls us to cultivate empathy. Disgust can motivate us to care for ourselves and others by setting healthy habits, maintaining appropriate boundaries, and fostering compassion toward suffering.

Jesus walked in uncomfortable places without fear of social or moral contamination. Walking with God means acting as agents of transformation—*eucontaminants* who cultivate healing rather than harm. Empathy leads to the heart of a caring God, whose love is the most contagious force of all.

Yuck Walking is a fun way of exploring how disgust influences your actions and reactions. You can Yuck Walk anywhere—poke a toe in mud, dip a finger into tree sap, or sniff a handful of soil. Consider caring for the earth by picking up litter or pulling invasive weeds. Step out of your comfort zone by wandering through a new part of town or dining at a restaurant serving unfamiliar foods. Remember to respect your limits: engage disgust thoughtfully and avoid overwhelming your senses. Practice curiosity and care as you walk with infectious love.

WALK IT OUT

Scripture Meditation

Read John 9:1-7. Focus phrase: *Jesus engages disgust with care.*

Walking Meditation

Before you go:

- Choose any path where you can encounter disgust with thoughtfulness and care.

As you walk:

- **Feel**. Pay attention to what makes you feel disgusted and how disgust makes you feel.
- **Notice** what disgust is trying to do, what it protects, and how it establishes boundaries.
- **Examine** how disgust moves you toward or away from God. Confess feelings of disgust toward a person, thing, or group. Consider how to respond with greater empathy.
- **Reorient** disgust toward care. How does Jesus' story inspire you to care for yourself and others? How might that be perceived as threatening?

Rest and Reflect

After your walk, reflect on this question: *How can I shift from fearing contamination to spreading love and care?*

WALK 13

Walk Before Dawn

Exploring Surprise

Take surprise out of faith and all that is left is dry and dead religion.

MICHAEL YACONELLI, *DANGEROUS WONDER*

EVERY SPRING, WHILE AMERICAN YOUTH gathered in churches for all-night lock-ins, my father rallied the youth of our Japanese mission for an all-night hike up Mount Asama. During my sister Kathy's senior year, she looked forward to her last mountain hike and the electrifying joy of watching the rising sun explode across Japan while peering into the yawning mouth of an active volcano. But midway through, pain from an old injury flared through her hip, forcing her to stop and rest. As the group pressed on toward the summit sunrise, my sister and a friend sank against a rock in a canyon feeling dark with disappointment.

Some surprises are joyful. Other surprises are devastating. The seventeenth-century Japanese poet Mizuta Masahide illustrated the paradox of surprise in a famous haiku: *My cottage burned down. I now own a better view of the rising moon.* Through the paradox of surprise, we are offered a fresh perspective. As the moon rose overhead, Kathy released her expectations of adventure and embraced stillness.

At daybreak, an unexpected flood of sunlight spilled over a ridge and burst the canyon wall into flaming light. Tingles rippled up Kathy's spine as radiance swallowed darkness. With renewed strength, she stretched and carefully followed the dewy scent of larch leaves into a verdant valley awash with crimson, yellow, and blue wildflowers. The breathtaking experience echoed the words of another seventeenth-century poet, Matsuo Basho: *How I long to see among dawn flowers the face of God.* Though Kathy enjoyed many mountaintop experiences, the surprising discovery of a beautiful mountain canyon at dawn bore a resemblance to the face of God that she will never forget—a face she has been chasing ever since.

Surprise is the most formational emotion. In their book *Surprise,* "surprisologists" Tania Luna and LeeAnn Renninger explain that the initial jolt of surprise amplifies other associated emotions by 400 percent, releasing a surge of intense feelings like elation, terror, bewilderment, or despair. The power of surprise upends expectations and strips away false beliefs about ourselves, others, and God. It also reveals hidden opportunities, fresh insights, and the wonder of God in unexpected places. The memory of surprising moments, like my sister's, lingers for years with crystal clarity.

We need surprise to learn, grow, and make meaningful sense of the world. Yet, because of its emotional complexity and intensity, surprise can be traumatic for individuals who struggle with sensory or emotional regulation. Recognizing the sensory impact and emotional intensity of surprise, we can practice compassion and calming strategies when needed.

To harness the power of surprise, Luna and Renninger suggest four movements: freeze, find, shift, and share. First, surprise causes a freeze response, which slows us down to discern if the situation presents an opportunity or danger. After the initial shock, surprise seeks to find meaning. By shifting perspective and releasing expectations, surprise leads to unexpected discoveries and new possibilities. Sharing our experience solidifies the new reality and enhances our connection to others.

Walking at dawn is an exhilarating way to start the day with a sense of surprise. You don't need to peer into a volcano to experience surprise; simply embrace the liminal space of dawn. Allow it to awaken your senses, focus your mind, and reveal something new. Daybreak holds a special numinous quality as creation unveils a new day—mist rises from the water like a shroud, fog blurs the sharp edges of treetops, bullfrogs croak their last goodnights, and trilling warblers greet the dawn.

Exposure to early morning light can help ward off depression by energizing your mind, lifting your mood, and brightening your perspective. Be mindful of the heightened emotions that arise with surprise and reflect on the assumptions that surprise seeks to challenge. Ask questions like *What opportunity is here? What can I release? How might this experience nurture faith, hope, and love?*

As you walk in the morning light, observe the shifts in shadows, colors, sounds, and smells. Stay open and curious, for each transformation carries a surprise—an opportunity to witness and discover the emergence of something new and to *chase the face of God among dawn flowers.*

WALK IT OUT

Scripture Meditation

Read Luke 24:1-12. Focus phrase: *At dawn, they found the tomb empty.*

Walking Meditation

Before you go:

- Choose a safe path for walking in the dark.
- Bring essentials like a flashlight or phone.

As you walk:

- **Awaken** your senses—notice shifts in light, sound, and smell. Consider listening to Nina Simone's "I'm Feeling Good" as a wake-up song.
- **Freeze** when something catches your attention. Notice the emotions surprise amplifies.
- **Find** meaning by embracing curiosity. How does the surprise make sense or evoke wonder?
- **Shift** your perspective by turning in a circle and exploring new perspectives. What assumptions, biases, or expectations can you shift? In what ways can you adapt to change and reorient to God's love?
- **Share** your experience with someone. Consider writing a haiku or taking a photo.

Rest and Reflect

After your walk, reflect on this question: *How can I discover new opportunities and chase the face of God in today's surprises?*

WALK 14

Walk in the Park

Exploring Fear

The most frequent command in the Bible is: Don't be afraid. Don't be afraid. Fear not. Don't be afraid . . . until you learn to live without fear you won't find it easy to follow Jesus.

N. T. WRIGHT, *FOLLOWING JESUS*

IN THE OPENING SCENE of the movie *The Mission*, a man tied to a cross plunges over a waterfall and plummets into white mist hundreds of feet below. The scene haunted me during my visit to Iguazu Falls. Due to my fear of heights, I opted to explore the jungle paths around the falls, refusing to walk the metal catwalk that extends over the rushing river where that dramatic scene was filmed. But when the trail behind us closed, a park ranger prodded us onto the catwalk toward the thunderous edge of the falls. The only way out was forward. Dizzied by the brown water surging beneath my feet, I gripped the cold handrail as fear trickled down my spine. Inching toward the precipice, *The Mission's* opening scene flooded my mind—except it was me plunging to impending doom.

Meanwhile, my daughter joyfully flitted along the walkway. I marveled that we could travel the same path with vastly different experiences. Sensing my fear, she took my hand and walked beside me until I felt calm and safe. With her loving support, I challenged and overcame my fear.

Fear is a survival instinct that prepares the body to fight, flee, or freeze when it perceives danger: racing pulse, rapid breathing, sweat, and hyperalertness. However, excessive fear can impair mental and physical health, memory, and judgment, according to researchers Lei Wang and colleagues in *Frontiers of Behavioural Neuroscience*. Often irrational, fear distorts reality, clings to false narratives, and fosters doubt in God's care. Unrecognized fear can fuel acts of violence and oppression.

Ignatius cautioned that fear's primary advisor is the enemy—any spirit or force that drives us away from God. However, love casts out fear (1 Jn 4:18) and trusts that nothing can separate us from God's love (Rom 8:38-39). According to bell hooks in *All About Love*, the choice to love moves us "against fear—against alienation and separation. The choice to love is a choice to connect—to find ourselves in the other."

Moving against fear doesn't have to be scary. A simple walk in the park is a surprisingly powerful way to examine and challenge our fear in a safe space. According to a study published by Simone Grassini in the *Journal of Clinical Medicine*, walking in nature improves mental health and effectively reduces anxiety. A peaceful stroll through a natural setting calms the body by activating the vagus nerve, reducing stress hormones that fuel anxiety, and releasing mood-boosting chemicals in the brain.

While the anxiety-reducing benefits of walking are significant, this spiritual wayfinding meditation is not meant to replace therapy. Instead of trying to conquer or cure fear, the invitation is to notice and challenge our fear with God's help. Facing our fear begins with naming it and examining its effect on our bodies, minds, and actions. We can resist fear by recalling God's past care, challenging irrational thoughts, and setting small achievable goals. If fear disrupts your emotional or mental state, seek support and counsel.

We are not meant to face fear alone. When my daughter took my hand at Iguazu Falls, I learned that fear diminishes when acknowledged in safe company, gestures of care dispel anxiety, and extending a hand transforms fear into courage. While Iguazu Falls is magnificent and terrifying, there is no stronger force than divine love channeled through human connection. As you walk, visualize Isaiah's description of God guiding you by the hand.

When fear arises, take steps to reorient to the current of love. If you don't know what to pray, use this prayer from Saint Augustine's *Confessions*:

> O Lord my God, tell me what you are to me. Say to my soul, I am your salvation. Say it so that I can hear it. My heart is listening, Lord; open the ears of my heart and say to my soul, I am your salvation. Let me run toward this voice and seize hold of you.

WALK IT OUT

Scripture Meditation

Read Isaiah 41:8-14. Focus phrase: *Do not fear, the LORD holds your hand.*

Walking Meditation

Before you go:

- Select a path through a park.
- Ask God to highlight a fear you can prayerfully examine.

As you walk:

- **Feel.** Gently twist your upper body, look over your shoulder, and recognize that you are safe.
- **Examine** your fear as you walk. Notice how it feels in your body, mind, and emotions, recognizing your impulse to fight, flee, or freeze. Does your fear move you toward or away from God?
- **Challenge** your fear by recalling times of God's faithfulness, exploring new perspectives, or setting achievable goals. If overwhelming thoughts arise, gently refocus on the present.
- **Orient** to God's love, envisioning God holding your hand. What strength and courage can you receive?

Rest and Reflect

After your walk, reflect on this question: *What steps can I take to transform fear with love?*

PART 3

Becoming Aware of Your Thoughts

Take, Lord, and receive all of my independence,
memory, understanding, and my entire will
—all of my resources and possessions.
You gave them to me. I return them to you.
Everything is yours. I entrust all of it to your care.
Only inflame my soul with your love and grace.
That is enough for me.

ST. IGNATIUS, "SUSCIPE," FROM THE *SPIRITUAL EXERCISES*, TRANSLATED BY DEBORAH GREGORY

WALK 15

Poohsticks

Releasing Sticky Thoughts

When you are a Bear of Very Little Brain, and you Think of Things, you find sometimes that a Thing which seemed very Thingish inside you is quite different when it gets out into the open and has other people looking at it.

WINNIE-THE-POOH IN A. A. MILNE'S *THE HOUSE AT POOH CORNER*

LOST IN A DAYDREAM, Winnie-the-Pooh walked across the bridge at the forest's edge and tripped. "Bother," said Pooh as the pine cone he held tumbled into the water. Pooh lay on the bridge, watching the water drift by, when suddenly, his pine cone drifted by too! Curiously, Pooh dropped pine cones and sticks over one side of the bridge and raced to the other to see which reappeared first. In A. A. Milne's children's book *House at Pooh Corner*, that's how Pooh invented the game *Poohsticks*, which he loved to play with his friends on Poohsticks Bridge.

One day, while playing Poohsticks, Roo fretted that his stick was stuck. "Rabbit, my stick's stuck. Is your stick stuck, Piglet?" Just then, something gray emerged from under the bridge. Rabbit chanted, "Come on, stick! Stick, stick, stick!" But, to his surprise, it was not a stick—it was Eeyore, who had fallen in the river and got caught up in a little eddy. Eeyore called for help before realizing that he could swim to shore. The friends played more Poohsticks, which Eeyore mostly won by tossing his stick in a twitchy sort of way.

With Pooh's friends in mind, my daughter and I tried a game of *Thought Poohsticks* at a local park. While searching for sticks, we noticed that the physical qualities of our sticks seemed to match the various sizes, weights, or textures of our thoughts. Then, by assigning thoughts to our sticks, we became acutely aware of how sticky our thoughts can be. Once we reached a bridge, we released our Thought Poohsticks into the water, relinquished control, and watched them float away.

Pooh's friends offer helpful lessons for playing Thought Poohsticks. Pooh releases thoughts that trip him up. Roo tells others when thoughts get stuck, and Rabbit cheers on positive thoughts. Piglet recognizes that not all thoughts are true or what they seem. Eeyore reminds us that we are not our thoughts, and when caught in a thought eddy, we can call for help or swim to shore. For us, as with Pooh's friends, releasing sticky thoughts gets easier with practice.

The psalmist declares that God knows us intimately and observes the flow of our thoughts (Ps 139:1-18). We can join God on Poohsticks Bridge to cast our anxious *thought sticks* into the water, remembering that God cares for us (1 Pet 5:7). Acknowledging and examining our most difficult thoughts in God's presence is safe.

To play Thought Poohsticks, select a path with a footbridge or approach to water. If water isn't accessible, adapt by throwing leaves in the wind or dropping twigs from a park bench. Acknowledge God's presence as you walk, noticing the thoughts that flow through your mind without judgment. When a thought troubles you, find a stick representing its weight, texture, or size. Respect the environment by only collecting what has fallen.

Approaching the water's edge, observe the current and how it mirrors your mind's flow. Assign a thought to a stick and toss it upstream. Notice what it feels like to release that thought and watch it float away. Try dropping two thought sticks simultaneously and observe how they move differently. If a thought returns, release it again with another stick, accepting that thoughts will come and go.

After releasing all your thought sticks, reflect on your feelings and spiritual insights. Notice what thoughts draw you to God or drift you away. Consider sharing your stickiest thoughts with a wise friend or counselor. Remember that Thought Poohsticks doesn't condemn difficult thoughts. Instead, it's a practice of acknowledging and releasing difficult thoughts in God's loving company. And as the last stick floats away, quiet your mind and listen for God's thoughts about you. They are vast, precious, and abounding in love.

WALK IT OUT

Scripture Meditation

Read Psalm 139:1-18. Focus phrase: *God intimately knows my thoughts.*

Walking Meditation

Before you go:

- Choose a path with a bridge or safe approach to water. Alternately, pick a path with leaves or twigs to toss in the wind.

As you walk:

- **Collect** sticks to symbolize sticky thoughts you want to release.
- **Observe** the water flow as you reflect on the flow of your thoughts.
- **Release** the sticks you have assigned with sticky thoughts and watch them float away. Observing how each stick behaves, consider how your thoughts draw you closer to God or drift you away.
- **Remember** the words of Psalm 139, imagining God's Spirit encircling and laying a hand on you. Consider listening to Christy Nockels's 2017 song "River of Grace."

Rest and Reflect

After your walk, reflect on this question: *What vast, wonderful, and precious thoughts does God think about me and creation?*

WALK 16

Labyrinth Walking

Untangling Fantasy and Rumination

To make a deep physical path, we walk again and again. To make a deep mental path, we must think over and over the kind of thoughts we wish to dominate our lives.

WILFRED ARLAN PETERSON, *THE ART OF LIVING, DAY BY DAY*

As AN AMBITIOUS YOUNG MAN, Ignatius craved the power, wealth, and influence of court life in the sixteenth century. However, after a cannonball shattered his leg in battle, Ignatius lay bedridden for months, grappling with the crushing reality that his military career and dreams of court life might also be shattered. To bide time, Ignatius requested novels about knightly chivalry and romance. But to his dismay, he received books about the life of Christ and the saints.

With nothing to do but daydream and read, Ignatius began to track the flow of his thoughts and how they impacted his mood. When fantasizing about war, fame, and sex, he felt gratified in the moment but sad and empty later. However, he found that meditating on the life of Christ and the saints brought him lasting joy.

This realization sparked a desire for Christ and a quest to follow the saints, culminating in a profound conversion experience.

While bedridden, Ignatius learned to resist fantasizing, but after his conversion, his mind spiraled into a dark state of scrupulous rumination on his former sins. Eventually, his priest refused to hear any more confessions from his past, pointing out that even religious thoughts can tangle our mind in knots if they lure us away from God's present grace. With these insights, Ignatius developed a habit of prayerfully examining his thoughts alongside his mood several times a day.

Centuries later, research confirms that indulging in thought patterns like fantasy and negative rumination can adversely affect mental health. In a journal article titled "Positive Future-Oriented Fantasies and Depressive Symptoms," psychologist Natalia Macrynikola and colleagues caution that while creative imagination and purposeful reflection can enhance well-being and assist in achieving goals, fantasizing—even about positive outcomes—can ultimately lead to feelings of depression and lower motivation over time.

Ignatius's insights help me recognize when my thoughts tangle in knots. When fantasizing, I spiral inward with self-indulgent thoughts that make me feel powerful and desirable. Fantasy escapes the present, distorts reality, and amplifies disappointment. Overthinking causes me to feel trapped in a maze of anxious thoughts. This brooding type of rumination rejects the here and now by fixating on the *what ifs* and *if onlys* of past or future scenarios. These thought loops tangle me in anxious dead-end thinking. Like Ignatius, my most dangerous mind knot is scrupulosity—an obsessive rumination on my sins, faults, and unworthiness. By feigning righteousness, scruples bend me away from God's grace and twist me inward into self-condemnation.

Instead of dwelling on *what if,* God desires that we find grace in *what is.* What *is* is God, who *is* full of endless love and mercy. I cannot follow the God who *is* by dwelling on the past or future. To walk with God is to take one step at a time with the *Great I Am* in this present moment.

A labyrinth is a winding geometric path used since early Christian times for prayer and discernment. Like a ball of yarn, a prayer labyrinth follows a single, continuous line with only one way in and out—there are no wrong turns or dead ends. Walking through its twists and turns helps to unravel mind knots, loosen restrictive thinking, and weave fresh perspectives. This prayer walk unfolds in three stages: unwind, re-center, and return.

Unwind a mind knot or simply allow your mind to wander as you follow the path. If you get lost in fantasy or rumination, draw your attention back to the present. Notice how your thoughts affect your body and emotions; slow down if you feel dizzy.

Re-center at the center, engaging your senses to help you focus on *what is* in the present moment. Reorient any *what if* and *if only* thoughts to *what is* true, noble, right, pure, lovely, admirable, and excellent (Phil 4:8).

Return by retracing your steps through the labyrinth. Accept that God's grace reaches you where you are and will carry you to where you need to go in due time. As you exit, remember that the God who *is* walks with you as a companion and guide.

WALK IT OUT

Scripture Meditation

Read Philippians 4:4-9. Focus phrase: *Think on what is.*

Walking Meditation

Before you go:

- Find a labyrinth near you at labyrinthlocator.org, or create your own by unwinding a ball of string. Follow the prompt to *unwind* as you unravel the ball, *re-center* as you reach the end of the string, and *return* as you wind it back up.

As you walk:

- **Remember,** the labyrinth is safe; you can't get lost. Ask God to guard your heart and mind.
- **Unwind** your mind knot, noticing how rumination and fantasy affect your body and mood.
- **Re-center** thoughts on *what is* true, noble, right, pure, lovely, admirable, and excellent.
- **Return**, remembering that God *is* your companion and guide.

Rest and Reflect

After your walk, reflect on this question: *What present grace helps me trust God's guidance and care?*

WALK 17

Creative Imagination

Making Nature Art

Perhaps imagination is only intelligence having fun.

GEORGE SCIALABBA IN *HARVARD MAGAZINE*

"LET'S MAKE A NATURE MANDALA," I suggested while wandering through our local art museum garden with my daughters Alina and Maggie. Making nature art is a fun way to exercise creativity. So is going for a walk. Research suggests that if you need a creative boost, go for a walk! According to a Stanford study, "Give Your Ideas Some Legs," published in the *Journal of Experimental Psychology*, Marily Oppezzo and Daniel Schwartz demonstrate that walking jogs the free flow of ideas and boosts creativity by 60 percent.

As we ambled through the garden, collecting fallen twigs, ferns, blossoms, berries, and leaves, I marveled that our movements can generate the creative imagination and problem-solving mindset needed to make art. Once we collected six of everything, we organized them into piles on a flat surface. Using a large pinecone as the centerpiece, we arranged it with purple beautyberries, twig spokes, and a ring of golden leaves. By placing the remaining items in concentric circles with repeating patterns, we began to create a fractal.

Fractals are abundant in nature—found in the symmetrical veins of leaves, the spiraling folds of flower petals, and the scaling sizes of fern fronds. Richard Taylor, a physicist at the University of Oregon who studies fractals, shared with *Oregon News* that observing nature can trigger a series of positive physiological responses, including reducing stress by 60 percent. Additionally, viewing nature while walking enhances divergent thinking and creativity.

Stepping back to admire our work of art, I laughed at the realization that we created a fractal-shaped mandala with fractal-patterned natural items—a fractal of fractals! My daughters and I noticed creativity can work like mandala making by reordering available resources in surprising, purposeful, and satisfying ways. We recognized that everyone has unique talents, skills, and resources to contribute toward building a more beautiful and just world. Then, Maggie raised an intriguing question: "If our life is like a mandala, what should we place at the center?" Alina wisely answered that putting ourselves at the center is human nature. However, self-centered creativity only benefits us and lacks beauty. "Only God can hold the tension of being at the center," she said.

The pinecone centerpiece reminded me of the tabernacle at the center of the Israelite camp. The people arranged their tents in concentric circles around the tabernacle, like a mandala. Each person contributed resources to build the sanctuary, and the Spirit of God filled them with creativity to construct a magnificent tent for God's glory and the cohesion of the community.

Our creativity is a gift that reflects God's own creativity and invites our participation in God's ongoing creative work in the world. Drawing from our imagination, self-expression, and personal resources, we cultivate wonder, healing, and meaningful connections for the greater good and God's glory. Circling our nature mandala, my daughters and I recognized its temporary and frail nature. We whispered a prayer of gratitude for the wonder of creation and creativity. Slowly, we walked away, hoping our nature mandala would surprise, delight, and inspire all who encountered it before the wind and squirrels returned our masterpiece back to the earth.

To create nature art while on a walk, bring a bag to collect natural materials like leaves, twigs, acorns, or flowers. Gather a similar number of each item and respect nature by only taking what has naturally fallen. Allow the outward focus of searching for available materials to illuminate the outward and inward focal points of your life. Reflecting on your life, what imagination do you have for the future? What skills and resources do you already have or need to move forward creatively?

When you're ready, find a flat surface to create a mandala. Begin by selecting one unique item as the centerpiece, and then carefully arrange groups of items around it to create concentric circles and spokes radiating outward. Aim for symmetry, but remember, there is no right or wrong way to make a mandala. Allow your unique resources, imagination, and perspective to flow naturally. Afterward, take time to appreciate your creation and consider what occupies the center of your life. Prayerfully consider how you can better utilize your talents and resources for the greater good and glory of God.

WALK IT OUT

Scripture Meditation

Read Exodus 35:4-21. Focus phrase: *Create with talent, skill, and resourcefulness.*

Walking Meditation

Before you go:

- Choose a path in a natural setting. Bring a bag to collect natural materials.
- Visit @jamesbruntartist on Instagram for creative inspiration.

As you walk:

- **Begin** with gratitude, acknowledging that creativity is a gift from God.
- **Collect** interesting natural materials that catch your eye, taking only what has fallen or is abundant.
- **Create** your mandala on a flat surface. Begin with an anchoring centerpiece and radiate concentric circles and spokes from the center. Strive for symmetry and balance.
- **Contemplate** your creation. Consider the central elements of your life and how well they hold tension. How might God become more central?

Rest and Reflect

After your walk, reflect on this question: *What resources and talents can I creatively exercise for God's glory and the greater good?*

WALK 18

Collecting Memory Stones

Recollecting Grace

Memories are the key not to the past, but to the future.

CORRIE TEN BOOM, *THE HIDING PLACE*

I HOPED TO EASE a painful childhood memory by hiking to a mountain lookout. Dark storm clouds loomed over the mountain as I reflected on the challenging move from Japan to America when I was nine. In Japan, our home was filled with people and laughter, but in America, my parents worked long hours, leaving me feeling alone and afraid. The instability of that time triggered my first anxiety attack.

As the sky darkened, I remembered an afternoon when my younger self, whom I think of as Little Debby, was crying on the couch, feeling scared. Looking back at our younger selves with compassion can be a healing experience. So, I asked Jesus to join a conversation between my present self and Little Debby. In my mind's eye, Jesus comforted her, saying, "You will build a nest for others one day. For now, rest. I have made a nest for you." I caressed Little Debby's hair and added, "You may not see it now, but God is a gentle mother bird watching over you. You're going to be all right. God's nest is the best kind of home."

The clouds broke, and the rain began to fall. I hurried down the path when a bird's alarm call startled me. Following the sound to a nearby tree, I was shocked to see a mother bird fanning her wings, shielding three little chicks from the approaching storm and human intrusion. Tears mingled with the rain as I blessed the little birds. This sensory-rich encounter brought my difficult past experience into the present grace. At last, Little Debby found shelter in the nest of the holy family and received the blessing she needed.

The next morning, I returned to find the chicks peacefully sleeping. To commemorate my experience of God's care, I collected stones from a nearby stream and built a small rock pile called a *cairn*. After taking a picture, I returned the stones to the earth. Though my memory may fade, the message imprinted on my heart remains: God's nest is the best kind of home.

Memories are vital for wayfinding as they shape our sense of place, context, and identity. They are not just stored in our brains; our bodies also play a part in shaping and storing memories. Gentle movements, like walking, improve memory and reduce the risk of dementia. The sensations of lifting stones and rubbing off the dirt engage *sensory memory,* which bonds memory and emotion.

Using sensory memory, people throughout history have built cairns to mark boundaries and remember divine encounters. Biblical figures like Samuel and Jacob erected stones of remembrance to commemorate God's provision and promises. Cairns are memory stones that help us trust the past and confirm the way forward.

Building cairns reminds us to handle memories carefully. Memories are fragile, often unreliable, or sometimes hold trauma. Forgetting is scary; being forgotten is terrifying. By stacking and balancing stones, we can process and regulate emotions stored in our somatic memory. When memories deepen despair, the psalmist found consolation in remembering stories of God's goodness and grace—much like my experience with the bird nest.

As you walk, collect a handful of eye-catching stones. Engage your memory to recollect a significant moment—a milestone, resolution, or calling—when you experienced God's goodness. Feel the stones' weight, texture, and shape in your hands as you reflect on God's provision and grace in the experience. If you can't think of a personal experience, meditate on the story of God's salvation in Psalm 77.

When you are ready, build a cairn by placing a large, flat stone as the base, then stack and balance the remaining stones. Use three points of contact for stability. Press a word or phrase you want to remember on each stone. Finally, bless the cairn as a signpost you can return to whenever you need guidance or a reminder of God's care and provision.

Tip: Remember that tampering with official cairns or building your own on public land or parks is illegal because it can mislead hikers and harm nature. If you build a cairn on land other than your own, take a photo or sketch a drawing of your cairn and dismantle it when you are finished.

WALK IT OUT

Scripture Meditation

Read Psalm 77. Focus phrase: *I will remember your wonders.*

Walking Meditation

Before you go:

- Choose a path in a setting that feels meaningful.

As you walk:

- **Recollect** a significant moment when you experienced God's goodness.
- **Collect** a handful of stones of different shapes and sizes. Engage your senses, noticing texture and temperature as you reflect on your memory.
- **Build** from large to small, stacking and balancing the stones on one another. Press your hand on the stone as you say a word or phrase you want to remember.
- **Bless** the memory with gratitude. If on public land, dismantle the cairn when finished.

Rest and Reflect

After your walk, reflect on this question: *What do I want to remember when I look back on this cairn in the future?*

WALK 19

Getting Lost

Discovering the Prayer of Examen

Yours is an examen of love. Still, I am afraid . . . afraid of what may surface. Even so, I invite you to search me to the depths so that I may know myself—and you—in fuller measure. Amen.

RICHARD J. FOSTER, *PRAYER*

On my first backcountry camping trip with friends, we hastily set up camp before dashing down an overgrown trail to an overlook with a stunning sunset view. Bathed in golden light, we frolicked among the boulders as the sky burst with colors. But when darkness fell, anxiety set in—only one person had a flashlight.

Holding hands, we followed the single beam into the dark forest but lost the trail within minutes. Panicked, we stumbled over unfamiliar ground and debated our direction. The false familiarity of a large tree or common stump misled us as we floundered without a map or compass. We were lost. I murmured a flickering prayer for divine help. Then, miraculously, we stumbled upon our campsite. The elation of finding our way in the dark far surpassed the thrill of the overlook at sunset.

Getting lost—on the trail and in life—feels dangerous and unnerving. Disorientation feels most intense when we lose our surest bearings in life: lost loved ones, lost jobs, lost dreams, lost community, lost security. Phrases like *I feel lost*, *I'm at a loss*, *losing myself*, and *losing faith* capture the empty ache of loss where our most formidable decisions occur. When lost, our greatest desire is to find: find the trail, find water, find shelter, find help, find our way home.

Wilderness survivalists use the acronym *STOP* when they are lost, which stands for *stop*, *think*, *observe*, and *plan*. First, *stop* to relax, breathe, and calm down. Next, *think* about your journey, remembering how you got to your current location. Then *observe* landmarks, dangers, obstacles, and your physical, emotional, and mental state; signal for help. Finally, *plan* by prioritizing your needs for today and tomorrow, then choosing the best course of action.

Spiritual wayfinders use a similar process for navigating life. We are reminded that God loves to find lost things: *lost* coins, *lost* sheep, *lost* people. Luke describes Jesus' mission as coming to seek and save the *lost*. When we feel lost, we can stop and rest assured that God is not lost. God is present and wants us to find our way home.

The Prayer of Examen was Ignatius of Loyola's sixteenth-century survival plan that continues to guide spiritual wayfinders today. The Examen involves becoming aware of our senses, emotions, thoughts, and desires in prayer and attuning ourselves to God's guidance in our daily lives. Not only is the Examen helpful when we feel lost, but a regular practice of Examen prevents us from getting lost when life feels disorienting. By reflecting on our past experiences, we can better understand where we have been, where we currently are, and where we are headed. When we feel lost, the Examen reminds us that God is always near and wants us to find our way home.

Ignatius advised his companions to pray the Examen three times a day to reflect on the previous hours, days, or even longer periods such as weeks, months, or years. This practice is especially helpful for examining times of difficulty, disorientation, and loss. To remind myself of this process, I use the acronym TARP, which helps me pause, seek refuge in God's presence, and review my journey with divine guidance before moving forward. Here's how to do it:

> *Thanksgiving:* Relax, breathe, and become aware of God's presence with you. Express gratitude for his provisions.
>
> *Ask for light:* Seek the Holy Spirit's guidance and wisdom.
>
> *Review:* Reflect on your day or an experience, noting your emotional, physical, and mental states. Identify what drew you closer to God or pushed you away.
>
> *Plan:* Prioritize needs for today and tomorrow, then prayerfully choose the best course of action. Ask God to guide the way.

You don't need to get lost for this meditation. Rather, follow a trusted path while reviewing your day, life journey, or an experience of loss, following a trusted path. Practicing the Examen prayer along a familiar route can help you remember and use it when you feel lost. If you want to reflect on feelings of uncertainty or disorientation during a time of loss, consider exploring a well-marked trail that you haven't visited before or walking a labyrinth. Embrace the unease of new surroundings as you practice trusting the path. Allow the Examen to draw you into God's tent as you review your journey or loss. Remember that God is near and wants you to find your way home.

WALK IT OUT

Scripture Meditation

Read Luke 15:1-10. Focus phrase: *God loves to find lost things.*

Walking Meditation

Before you go:

- Select a familiar path or find a clearly defined trail that you haven't explored before.

As you walk:

- Relax and become aware of God's presence. Notice feelings of disorientation, uncertainty, or loss.
- Pray the Examen, reviewing your day or experience.
  - **Thanksgiving.** Express gratitude for God's provisions.
  - **Ask** for the Spirit's guidance and light.
  - **Review** your day or experience, noting your emotional, physical, and mental states. Identify what drew you closer to God or pushed you away.
  - **Plan** what you need for tomorrow. Ask for God's help.

Rest and Reflect

After your walk, reflect on this question: *Where did I sense God's presence most clearly, and where did I feel most distant or resistant?*

PART 4

Spiritual Orienteering

God's love overflows into creation and extends to me. I was created to walk with God and orient my life toward God's love. My essential purpose is to grow and flourish in God's love and cultivate good fruit for the life of the world. Every gift of creation is helpful for navigating a purposeful path. By stewarding these gifts for God's glory and the good of others, I experience freedom and flourishing. However, if I become attached to anything that diverts me from love, I lose my way and stray from my true purpose. Along life's path, I aim for balance and a healthy indifference to outcomes—not fixing my heart's compass on health or sickness, wealth or poverty, honor or disgrace, or a long life or a short one. All things can direct my life toward God's love and evoke a deeper expression of love within me. At every turn, let my only desire and choice be whatever orients my life toward God's love and flourishes the life of the world.

"THE GUIDING FRAMEWORK FOR SPIRITUAL ORIENTEERING," ADAPTED FROM THE FIRST PRINCIPLE AND FOUNDATION OF SAINT IGNATIUS, TRANSLATION AND ADAPTATION BY DEBORAH GREGORY

WALK 20

Navigating with Trees

Orienting to Divine Love

God's love overflows into creation and extends to me.
I was created to walk with God and orient my life toward God's love.
My essential purpose is to grow and flourish in God's love
and cultivate good fruit for the life of the world.

ADAPTED AND TRANSLATED BY DEBORAH GREGORY FROM THE FIRST PRINCIPLE AND FOUNDATION OF SAINT IGNATIUS

IN THE QUIET OF THE NIGHT, I slipped on my shoes, pushed open the creaky retreat center door, and searched for east—the direction of sunrise. Unable to find my bearings in the darkness, I looked to the crescent moon for guidance. By tracing a line from the upper to lower horns of the moon and continuing down to the horizon, I found south.

Turning left, I walked eastward until I encountered a large moonlit statue of Jesus with one arm stretched to heaven, and the other to earth. As the eastern sky brightened, the golden sun rose and filled Christ's lower hand. I stood in awe as the ascending sun slowly traced Christ's body, formed a stunning halo around his head, and then enveloped his upward-reaching hand in glowing light. Astonished, I recalled Jesus' words: "I am the light of the world. Whoever follows me will never walk in darkness but will have the light of life" (Jn 8:12).

The first principle of spiritual wayfinding is that God loves us and created us to walk in the light and to produce good fruit for the world. Just as trees flourish by facing the sun, we thrive by orienting our lives toward divine light. Spiritual wayfinders seek signs of God's light and orient their lives toward it.

Before modern tools like GPS, navigators relied on natural elements like the sun, moon, and stars. In *The Natural Navigator,* Tristan Gooley explains how to navigate using trees by observing how they grow toward the light. I stood among the trees as their long shadows stretched and yawned westward. They would become my teachers as I practiced natural navigation.

I noticed that leaves and branches grow denser where they receive the most sunlight. Because I was in the northern hemisphere, where the sun travels across the southern sky, denser limbs and foliage tend to extend horizontally toward the south. In contrast, shadier northern branches tend to stretch upward for light. These growth patterns are most evident in isolated trees not competing for light.

Lying in the grass under a tree, I admired how each leaf grew purposefully. Smaller, brighter sun leaves act like solar panels at the crown and sunny southern side, while longer, darker shade leaves collect diffused light on the northern and lower limbs. I marveled at their adaptability and resourcefulness.

Despite these useful directional signs, Gooley warns wayfinders not to assume direction based on a single sign. Many factors shape and distort a tree's growth. For instance, smaller trees may slant to reach sunlight, and shaded trees may bend toward light reflected off surfaces like water or windows. Natural navigators must pay attention to a tree's response to the availability or limitation of resources.

I stood and stretched before walking back for breakfast. On my way, I stopped at the statue of Jesus to reflect on my life. I want to emulate Jesus and the trees—intentionally reaching toward heaven while rooting deeply in the earth. Like many small trees, I've experienced slow growth under the shadow of dominating trees and cultural influences, but I am resourceful and resilient. God's light reaches me through gaps in the canopy and unexpected reflective surfaces. How can I grow, change, or adapt to live more fully in God's light? How can I make space for divine light to reach others? My deepest desire is to illuminate and reflect the light of Christ each new day.

This meditation encourages you to practice these principles while navigating with trees as your guide. Observe how trees orient to the light by looking for density patterns and leaf shape. As you walk, reflect on the orientation of your life and how God might be inviting you to reorient, grow, and flourish.

WALK IT OUT

Scripture Meditation

Read John 8:12. Focus phrase: *Walk in the light of life.*

Walking Meditation

Before you go:

- Choose a path among trees.

As you walk:

- **Stretch** and bend as you face the light.
- **Observe** how trees orient toward the light.
- **Tree growth.** Notice signs of asymmetrical growth with denser leaf and branch growth on the sunnier southern side. Southern limbs tend to grow more horizontally, and northern limbs more vertically; these trends are opposite in the southern hemisphere.
- **Sun and shade leaves.** Look for smaller, brighter, and thicker sun leaves growing on the top and south-facing side of trees, and larger, darker, and thinner shade leaves growing on the shadier north-facing side.
- **Consider** your orientation and growth patterns.

Rest and Reflect

After your walk, reflect on this question: *How might I grow, change, or adapt to live more richly in divine light?*

WALK 21

Pattern Spotting

Finding Signs of God Everywhere

Every gift of creation is helpful for navigating a purposeful path. By stewarding these gifts for God's glory and the good of others, I experience freedom and flourishing.

ADAPTED AND TRANSLATED BY DEBORAH GREGORY FROM THE FIRST PRINCIPLE AND FOUNDATION OF SAINT IGNATIUS

MY DAUGHTER ALINA HAS a fascination with math and spotting patterns. During a recent walk, we observed that nature seldom presents the straight lines and smooth circles she's taught in geometry class. Instead, flowers emerge as pinwheels, acorn-cap scales radiate into mandalas, and creepy eyeball shapes spiral up sabal palm trees.

Fascinated by the wild complexity of the natural world, mathematician Benoit Mandelbröt searched for traces of order in the seemingly chaotic rough edges. Astonishingly, he discovered that "each part is like the whole but smaller," as he explained in a TED-Ed talk. His keen interest in spotting rough patterns led to the development of fractal geometry, which has applications in weather prediction, AI training, and designing retinal implants.

A fractal is a complex pattern that repeats itself in different sizes. The smallest parts resemble the largest ones, no matter how zoomed in or out. Finding fractals can be both enjoyable and beneficial.

Richard Taylor, a physics professor at the University of Oregon, told BBC's *Deep Calm* podcast that humans are wired to seek the symmetry and flow of fractal patterns. Discovering fractals while walking in nature can recharge the mind and reduce stress by up to 60 percent.

Alina and I often search for fractals during our walks by following the advice that Mandelbröt offers in his memoir, *The Fractalists*: "When I seek, I look, look, look." The universe abounds with self-replicating patterns, from intricate snowflakes to spiraling galaxies. We discover fractals in flowers, ferns, seashells, and dead tree branches forking into smaller limbs and twigs. As I lifted a flower stem, Alina pointed to one on my finger. Gazing at my fingerprint, I marveled at the astounding form and function of fractals within my body—spectacular impressions of God's life within me that connect me to all of creation.

While fractal spotting, Alina asked a stunning question: "What if we looked for God in our lives like we are looking for fractals?" The Bible encourages seeking: seek God and he will be found; seek first the kingdom of God; seek the kingdom like a hidden treasure. I tend to search for God in sacred places like the Bible and church, yet Scripture affirms that God fills the universe. What keeps me from discovering the impressions of God's life in all things?

Fractals remind us to trust God's order within the chaos and rough edges of life. They prompt us to "look, look, look" for God's creative presence everywhere, especially in ordinary and overlooked places. Finding God in all things requires openness to divine encounters in every aspect of our lives. God called to Moses from an ordinary bush; only when Moses approached to look at the burning bush did God speak. In her poem *Aurora Leigh*, Elizabeth Barrett Browning wrote:

> Earth's crammed with heaven,
> And every common bush afire with God;

But only he who sees takes off his shoes,
The rest sit round it and pluck blackberries.

By spotting patterns in nature, we uncover heaven crammed into earth, discovering patterns of love begetting love, life regenerating life, and justice wrapped in mercy. We may not see a burning bush, but even an ordinary blackberry bramble bears heaven's flame for those willing to draw close.

As you walk, observe repeating shapes in clouds, ferns, flowers, and seashells. Notice your physical and emotional reactions to these patterns found in ordinary places. After your walk, express your experience creatively—perhaps by drawing a fractal or writing a Fibonacci sequence poem.

The *Fibonacci sequence* is a pattern of expanding numbers formed by adding the two preceding numbers: 0, 1, 1, 2, 3, 5, 8, 13, and so on. In response to Elizabeth Barrett Browning's poem, I created a Fibonacci sequence poem using one syllable for the first and second lines, two syllables for the third line, and continuing this pattern until the poem ends on the seventh line with thirteen syllables. Feel free to experiment and create your own expressive patterns!

"Plucking Blackberries"
Deborah Gregory

bare
foot
earthing
blackberry
picking, plucking, plop
mouth crammed with heavenly juices
puckering lips dribbling drops from chin to my toes

WALK IT OUT

Scripture Meditation

Read Exodus 3:1-6. Focus phrase: *I will go over and see this strange sight.*

Walking Meditation

Before you go:

- Choose a nature path among trees or in a botanical garden.

As you walk:

- **Look** for patterns all around you. Step in closely to observe intricate details, then step back to appreciate the broader view. Look up and watch the clouds and look down to study a flower.
- **Notice** your physical and emotional response to discovering patterns.
- **Consider** your life. Where do you see signs of God at work in the ordinary aspects of life?
- **Respond** creatively by drawing a fractal or writing a poem using Fibonacci's sequence to capture your experience.

Rest and Reflect

After your walk, reflect on this question: *Where do I notice patterns of God's activity in my life?*

WALK 22

Tree-Eyes Trek

Pruning Attachments

By stewarding these gifts for God's glory and the good of others, I experience freedom and flourishing. However, if I become attached to anything that diverts me from love, I lose my way and stray from my true purpose.

ADAPTED AND TRANSLATED BY DEBORAH GREGORY FROM THE FIRST PRINCIPLE AND FOUNDATION OF SAINT IGNATIUS

THAT ONE HAS CAT EYES!" my daughter exclaimed as we passed a tall oak draped in scruffy Spanish moss. Finding tree faces is a favorite family pastime. We look for eye-shaped pruning scars, knot noses, bark-crack smiles, and lip-puckered knobs that form faces. We've even nicknamed a neighbor's oak "Gasping Gus" because its wide-eyed scars and raised limbs make it look surprised. I enjoy greeting his cheerful face during my neighborhood walks.

While searching for tree faces, my daughters noticed different types of pruning scars. Human-pruned branches leave round scars resembling human eyes. Self-pruned branches develop naturally when a tree restricts resources to a branch until it drops. This process forms oval-shaped callouses resembling cat eyes. My children call human-made scars *people eyes* and self-pruned scars *cat eyes*. Over time, *people eyes* will develop callouses that resemble *cat eyes*.

I am drawn to *cat-eyed* trees and their marvelous ability to self-prune! Tall forest trees with compact canopies excel at this form of self-care. In their quest for light, they naturally release unproductive branches and direct their energy upward. Self-pruning is a cooperative process that involves "acts of God" such as wind, snow, ice, and even animals climbing on the trees, all contributing to the natural process. Self-pruning allows a tree to thrive, while the decaying twigs that fall to the forest floor provide nourishment to the surrounding environment.

In contrast, trees rooted in spacious yards with abundant light tend to grow wide and full. However, they are less efficient at self-pruning than forest trees, and their heavy and over-extended limbs are more vulnerable to falling during storms. Trees like *Gasping Gus* benefit from the skillful hands of pruners to remain healthy.

I feel a lot like Gasping Gus. I tend to overextend myself believing that unlimited growth signifies freedom. Clutching each limb as necessary and good, I am slow to recognize when unhealthy attachments restrict growth or cause harm. Walking among forest trees reminds me that true freedom grows when I willingly release attachments that hinder upward growth.

"The Guiding Framework for Spiritual Orienteering," found at the beginning of section four, recognizes that everything in creation is a gift from God. How we hold and release these gifts profoundly impacts our sense of freedom.

In a talk at the Practice Church, Fr. Michael Sparough, SJ, emphasized that we often fail to recognize our unhealthy attachments until they are threatened. Life's storms reveal the factors that shape our identity, security, and purpose. We tend to cling to our jobs, health, successes, intellect, community, and relationships for our sense of identity. While these may be good gifts, relying on the security, power, affection, or approval they bring can hinder our growth and freedom. Jesus came to offer life and freedom: "I am the vine; you are the branches," he said. "Abide in my love" (Jn 15:5, 9). Healthy detachment frees us to grow closer to Jesus, the divine source of life.

Like Gasping Gus, I need help to discern where my growth is uneven and where I reach too ambitiously. I need a master gardener to prune away what is dead or diseased in me. Like forest trees, I want to quickly notice where I've grown wild, overextended, or when I overshadow others. When my children look at my life, I want them to see cat eyes—marks of purposeful detachment, character growth, true freedom, and the flourishing of God's life in me for the good of others.

Explore a path among the trees and look for signs of pruning. Look for tree faces and try to distinguish the *cat-eyed* self-pruning scars from *people-eyed* human pruning scars. Reflect on areas in your life where you need to let go, recognizing any unhealthy attachments. Allow the trees, along with "The Guiding Framework for Spiritual Orienteering," to lead you toward greater freedom and growth toward God's light.

WALK IT OUT

Scripture Meditation

Read John 15:5-11. Focus phrase: *Abide in love.*

Walking Meditation

Before you go:

- Choose a path among trees.

As you walk:

- **Observe** trees, noticing signs of human or natural pruning and the *tree faces* that give them character. Ask God to reveal where you need pruning or a deeper connection to God's life.
- **Consider** the gifts you most cherish. How do they shape your character? Are there gifts you hold onto too tightly that block the flow of divine life and love?
- **Practice this releasing exercise:**
    - ◇ Face the light and stretch your arms like a tree abiding in God's love.
    - ◇ Shake your arms and name what you want to release.
    - ◇ Sway gently, embracing flexibility and freedom. Express your intention to live more fully in God's love.

Rest and Reflect

After your walk, reflect on this question: *What can I practice releasing in order to grow in freedom and flourish in love?*

WALK 23

Windflüchter Walk

Navigating with Wind-Shaped Trees

Along life's path, I aim for balance and a healthy indifference to outcomes—not fixing my heart's compass on health or sickness, wealth or poverty, honor or disgrace, or a long life or a short one. All things can direct my life toward God's love and evoke a deeper expression of love within me.

ADAPTED AND TRANSLATED BY DEBORAH GREGORY FROM THE FIRST PRINCIPLE AND FOUNDATION OF SAINT IGNATIUS

IN THE SAME YEAR that Alexander Graham Bell patented the telephone and Lakota chiefs defeated Custer in the Battle of Little Bighorn, a hickory seed sprouted in Florida's sandy soil. As the world endured winds of technological and social change, the hickory faced strong eastern sea breezes and mighty hurricanes that bent its trunk as it grew. Today, the hickory bows across my front yard as a monument of resilience.

My leaning hickory is *windflüchter*—a German term for trees shaped by strong winds. A tree's response to wind stress determines its formation and resilience. My hickory, while bent by early life storms and years of prevailing winds, produces an abundance of nuts each year. She is healthy and strong because she grew firmly anchored roots and reaction wood. Windflüchter trees are living emblems of hope.

I enjoy searching for windflüchters on my woodland walks, looking for signs of adaptive growth in response to external pressures. Starting at the root collar, I look for thicker, longer structural roots on the wind-exposed side, stabilizing the tree by pointing toward the prevailing winds. Next, I examine the trunk for reaction wood, which forms in response to stress or uneven weight distribution. This wood appears thick or bulging where the trunk bends or where roots flare. Hardwood trees like oak and maple develop reaction wood on the wind-facing side, while conifers, such as pine and spruce, produce compression wood on the opposite side. Then I look up to see how flexibly the branches sway—flexible branches don't easily break during a storm.

Observing windflüchter trees encourages reflection on the forces shaping our lives. In *The Human Condition,* Cistercian monk Thomas Keating identifies three essential needs for healthy growth: security and survival, power and control, and affection and esteem. However, an overreliance on these needs can lead to a bent sense of self. Without confronting social pressures and our hidden motivations, our bent selves unconsciously influence our choices throughout life.

Walking among windflüchter trees teaches us valuable lessons about resilience and balance. Observing their roots sparks curiosity about the stabilizing forces in our lives. Examining reaction wood encourages reflection on how we respond to stress. Their flexibility reminds us to sway freely amid life's storms. When we rigidly cling to desired outcomes, we lack freedom and a genuine openness to God's will. True freedom cultivates balance—a rootedness in God's love that stabilizes us through life's storms and pressures. It prompts us to gauge the orientation of our hearts by asking *Am I driven by power, wealth, success, or reputation? Can I allow weakness, poverty, failure, or ridicule to deepen my experience of God's love in and through me?*

Like a windflüchter tree that adapts to pressure, we, too, can cultivate counterbalancing practices to stabilize our growth. Ignatius of Loyola proposed a method called *agere contra*, which encourages us to counteract our inclinations by *doing the opposite.* For example, when we feel the urge to take control under pressure, we might do the opposite by loosening our grip on outcomes. Or instead of people-pleasing, we can focus on our core values and what pleases God.

While walking under my bowed hickory after a recent storm, I realized my relentless bent toward certainty limits my ability to follow God when I can't control the outcomes. Although I cannot command the winds of change, I can lean against my hickory and appreciate its deep roots and thick reaction wood as it sways freely with the breeze. Today, I can take small counterbalancing measures: take a small risk, trust that I have enough, and breathe *yes* into the wind. With Ignatius, I can freely pray: *My one desire and choice is whatever orients my life toward the love of God and flourishes the life of the world.*

Search for windflüchter trees as you walk in a wooded area. When you find a bent tree, look for counterbalancing growth in its tree roots, reaction wood, and swaying branches. Reflect on the areas where you feel bent or pressured by life's storms. Consider the counterbalancing steps you can take to develop resilience and balance.

WALK IT OUT

Scripture Meditation

Read Matthew 14:22-33. Focus phrase: *When afraid, step out in trust.*

Walking Meditation

Before you go:

- Choose a path among trees.

As you walk:

- **Wind-direction check.** Wet your finger and turn in a circle. Your finger will feel colder when facing the wind.
- **Observe** leaning trees. Look for thicker, longer roots that point toward the prevailing winds. Examine the bark for counterbalancing signs of thick or bulging reaction wood. Observe the flexibility of the branches swaying in the wind.
- **Consider** the prevailing winds that shape your life. How rooted are you in God's love? Where do you lean away from God? What steps can you take to counterbalance your lean?
- **Breath prayer.** Facing each direction, exhale into the wind: *Yes, wherever you lead.*

Rest and Reflect

After your walk, reflect on this question: *How can I practice greater openness, flexibility, and freedom to follow God's leading?*

WALK 24

Desire Paths

Noticing the Way of the Heart

At every turn, let my only desire and choice be whatever orients my life toward God's love and flourishes the life of the world.

ADAPTED AND TRANSLATED BY DEBORAH GREGORY FROM THE FIRST PRINCIPLE AND FOUNDATION OF SAINT IGNATIUS

AT THE HEART OF The Ohio State University campus lies the iconic Oval, a vast green space marked by geometric paths that crisscross between academic buildings. When we lived in Columbus, my kids loved roaming the paths whenever we visited the campus. Originally, the Oval served as pastureland for grazing cows and sheep. As the university constructed buildings around the Oval, footpaths emerged organically, charting the most desirable routes between buildings. Eventually, these *desire paths*—also known as cow paths—were paved to facilitate easier movement.

In a viral social media post, nature writer Robert Macfarlane described desire paths as "free-will ways"—timeworn paths made by the "wishes & feet of walkers, especially those paths that run contrary to design or planning." Today, the Oval is a hubbub of free-will activity as people walk, skateboard, and ride bicycles along the paved paths. The grassy areas between paths provide open space for free-range activities like tossing frisbees, playing guitar, studying, and picnicking with friends. The campus community—and my family—delight in the beauty and efficiency of the Oval's enduring desire paths.

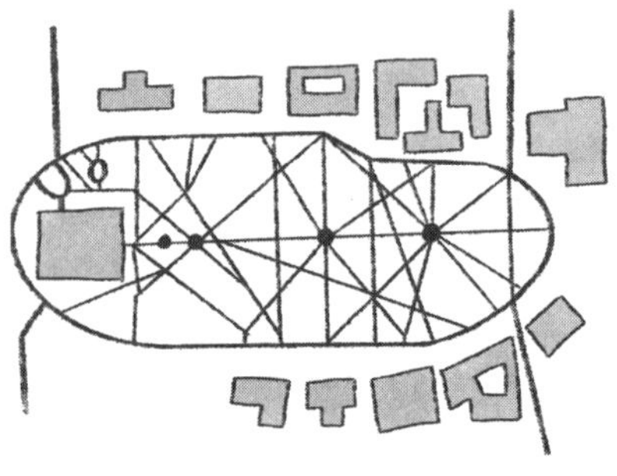

The Oval, as drawn by Alina Gregory

"Paved roads show us where we ought to go, but desire paths are made when we step off the road and let our hearts decide the way," states University of Edinburgh professor David Farrier in *Emergence Magazine*. These paths can reveal the hidden motivations and unexpressed yearnings that shape the landscape of our lives. When life's pathway becomes rugged or inefficient, we instinctively forge new paths—shortcuts and detours that let our hearts guide the way. Some desire paths, like those in the Oval, emerge from positive intentions that foster learning and social connection. Other desire paths develop from lazy habits or a sense of entitlement that leads to erosion, ruts, and hazards for ourselves and others.

Farrier describes desire paths as "no more than the trace of a decision—less than that, an impulse—to find a new way." I recognize this impulse when I bypass discomfort by clinging to feel-good platitudes instead of confronting difficult truths. At times, I seek escape routes when commitments feel too demanding. Occasionally, I take shortcuts to receive immediate praise rather than investing time in developing skills and character. My desire paths are most evident when I convince myself that the grass is greener elsewhere. Exploring desire paths during my walks helps me to dig deeper into the buried desires and hidden motivations that guide my choices.

Urban planners analyze desire paths to understand what motivates human choices. They examine where the trails lead, who created them, and what desires contributed to their development. By assessing the environmental impact of desire paths, they can determine when to pave beneficial routes and block detrimental ones.

Similarly, spiritual wayfinders examine the desire paths of our lives to uncover the impulses already guiding our decisions. Intentional examination of our desires strengthens our ability to discern when to stay on a particular path and when to leave it. "The Guidelines for Spiritual Orienteering," found at the beginning of part four, concludes with a simple but profound prayer: *At every turn, let my only desire and choice be whatever orients my life toward God's love and flourishes the life of the world.*

As you walk, look for desire paths around you. They are commonly found in places with heavy foot traffic, like parks, university campuses, shopping malls, and apartment complexes. Look for signs of thinning grass, compact soil, exposed roots, or gaps in bushes that veer off the main route. Desire paths often extend across fields, between buildings, or around parking lots.

Reflect on your life path. What shortcuts do you take for convenience? Where might you bypass challenges or trespass with a sense of entitlement? Consider the long-term effects your desire paths may have—both positively and negatively—on others and the world around you. Examine your heart, noticing how your impulses orient you toward God's love and the good of others. Each encounter with a desire path presents an opportunity to discern our seemingly insignificant choices and pray: *Where does love lead here?*

WALK IT OUT

Scripture Meditation

Read *Proverbs 16:1-3.* Focus phrase: *My way seems pure, but God weighs motives.*

Walking Meditation

Before you go:

- Choose a location with high pedestrian traffic, such as a park, university campus, or apartment complex.

As you walk:

- **Look** for desire paths and their features: Are they shortcuts or bypasses? What desires forged the path? What benefit or harm do they cause?
- **Reflect** on the desire paths you follow and your motivations: Do you prefer shortcuts or bypasses? What desires shape your habits? What benefit or harm do they cause?
- **Be intentional** about the paths you choose in life. What harmful path do you want to resist? What new path could you explore for the greater good?

Rest and Reflect

After your walk, reflect on this question: *What desires move me toward the love of God and the life of the world?*

PART 5

Exercising Discernment

Holy Spirit, you, light of our understanding, gentle breath that guides our decisions, grant me the grace to listen attentively to your voice and to discern the hidden paths of my heart, so that I may grasp what truly matters to you, and free my heart from its troubles. I ask you for the grace to learn how to pause, to become aware of the way I act, of the feelings that dwell within me, and of the thoughts that overwhelm me which, so often, I fail to notice. I long for my choices to lead me to the joy of the Gospel. Even if I must go through moments of doubt and fatigue, even if I must struggle, reflect, search, and begin again. . . . Because, at the end of the journey, your consolation is the fruit of the right decision. Grant me a deeper understanding of what moves me, so that I may reject what draws me away from Christ, and love him and serve him more fully. Amen.

PRAYER FOR FORMATION IN DISCERNMENT, READ BY POPE LEO XIV[1]

WALK 25

Bushwalking

The Courage to Want

I will not go where the path may lead,
but I will go where there is no path, and I will leave a trail.

MURIEL STRODE, *WIND-WAFTER WILDFLOWERS*

I FIRST MET KAYLA during a vision-collage session at a disability advocacy workshop. While sharing my collage, I felt brave naming a secret dream of writing a book. Kayla shared jokes and photos of food she dreamed of eating. Although Kayla's disability impacts motor skills and speech, she lands perfect jokes with her slow and steady voice. The next day, Kayla confessed to me a dream she hadn't shared on her collage: "I want to write worship songs and make music."

As women in different life stages, we connected over the shared apprehension and excitement of voicing what we want—the obstacle-ridden dreams that make us feel alive and purposeful. Kayla did something courageous by naming what she wanted—she allowed herself to dream. A year later, Kayla took her desire in a more daring direction than a recording studio; she took it to court. "I don't want guardianship anymore. I want supported decision-making," she told a judge. The right to make our own choices is a fundamental human right that is often denied to those with disabilities. While guardianship transfers decision-making authority to a guardian, supported decision-making empowers individuals with disabilities to make their own choices with the support of a trusted advisory team.

Kayla is not just a wayfinder—she's a bushwalker, fearlessly blazing new trails through challenging terrain. Bushwalking is an Australian pastime that involves exploring wild places and forging new paths. Usually walked with others, a bushwalk strengthens navigation skills, builds endurance, and fosters friendships. Bushwalking requires courage to reach a goal, honest self-assessment of limitations, resilience in facing challenges, and a commitment to sharing the journey. Bushwalkers always tell someone where they want to go and share their location along the way.

My favorite biblical bushwalker is Bartimaeus, a man with a visual disability whose story is told in Mark 10. When Bartimaeus heard Jesus approaching, he defiantly raised his voice to cry for mercy despite being silenced by those around him. Though he could not see, he courageously carved a path through the crowded street to reach Jesus.

Jesus then asked Bartimaeus the most important question we can pose to one another: "What do you want?" In response, Bartimaeus boldly expressed his seemingly impossible desire to see. By restoring Bartimaeus's sight, Jesus also renewed his sense of agency and his courage to want. Feeling vibrant and purposeful, Bartimaeus eagerly followed Jesus along a wild new road.

For many Christians, *desire* is a bad word. Yet Scripture affirms the goodness of desires that draw us to God and guide us on God's pathway of justice and mercy. By asking Bartimaeus what he wants, Jesus illustrated the revolutionary power and dignity of God-given human agency. Exploring our desires—discerning how they draw us to God, align with our core values, and contribute to the greater good—is the beginning of wisdom and human flourishing.

You don't need to hike the Australian bush to practice bushwalking; you can apply its principles anywhere. Together with Kayla and Bartimaeus, a spiritual practice of bushwalking can help you courageously explore your desires, confront challenges, and forge new paths as you follow Jesus. This practice unfolds in four steps.

First, choose a trail that is new or challenging for you. Allow the freshness, uncertainty, and obstacles of the path to help you reflect on your life's journey. Next, let yourself dream. Recall the dignity Jesus affirmed in Bartimaeus by asking, "What do you want?" What dreams ignite aliveness and purpose and inspire greater love, justice, and mercy?

Then, assess the challenges and obstacles you anticipate facing. How willing are you to leave the established path? What hinders or holds you back? As you weigh the movements of your heart, reflect on how pursuing your dream strengthens or diminishes your faith, hope, and love.

Finally, consider one small step you can take toward this dream. Repeat this walk as often as you need, closely examining how the movements of your heart draw you toward or away from God as you move forward. Remember, spiritual wayfinders commit to never bushwalking alone. Be sure to share your dream with companions and wise counselors. Seek God's confirmation, protection, and provision along the way.

WALK IT OUT

Scripture Meditation

Read Mark 10:46-52. Focus phrase: *What do you want?*

Walking Meditation

Before you go:

- Choose a new or challenging path, perhaps somewhere you have wanted to explore.

As you walk:

- **Notice.** How does it feel to walk a new or rugged path? Reflect on the established paths of your life.
- **Dream.** What do you want? What dreams animate you? Do they lead toward greater love, justice, and mercy?
- **Challenges.** Honestly assess the obstacles and challenges you will face. What hinders or holds you back?
- **Courage.** What small step can you take to move forward?
- **Share** your dreams with companions and seek God's guidance.

Rest and Reflect

After your walk, reflect on this question: *What desire or dream awakens faith, hope, and love in me?*

WALK 26

Walking with Prayer Pebbles

Discovering What's Important

Living into our values means . . . we walk our talk—we are clear about what we believe and hold important.

BRENÉ BROWN, *DARE TO LEAD*

WITHOUT A GREETING, the ENT doctor rushed into the room, switched on the noisy ear-suction machine, grabbed the sucker wand, and rolled her squeaky stool toward my daughter, who froze in terror. I leaped up to stop a procedure we didn't want. My daughter's sensory processing needs had been disregarded, and we needed to find a new doctor.

In a course on person-centered planning, my instructor, Laura Buckner, offered insight into experiences like my daughter's. Too often, what's important *for us* dictates what's important *to* us—especially for people with disabilities. According to Buckner, "We must work to find balance." Balancing the *for* and *to* of our desires empowers us to make wise and purposeful decisions.

Buckner suggested giving doctors a "One Sheet" describing my daughter's sensory processing differences and highlighting her desires with boxes labeled: *Important for Me* and *Important to Me*. While it's important *for* her to have healthy ears, it's equally important *to* her that her sensory experience is understood, her body respected, and that she is included in treatment decisions.

After I gave a new doctor the One Sheet, he calmly entered the room, knelt at eye level with my daughter, and gently asked, "What do you want me to do for you today?" His actions balanced my daughter's needs and desires, allowing her to feel seen, safe, and dignified. It reminded me of the tender way Jesus asked Bartimaeus, "What do you want me to do for you?" Desire often carries a negative stigma, but acknowledging our desires can protect against abuse and harm.

Growing up, I learned that Christian women should deny their desires and serve others. I didn't know how to express my needs or pursue my desires without feeling selfish. Teaching my daughter to discern and advocate for her needs and desires would require me to learn to do it myself.

Inspired by a neighbor who enjoys walking with prayer beads, I picked up a few pebbles and acorns to pass between my fingers as I walked. Ancient Christians used pebbles, knotted ropes, and prayer beads to connect the body and heart in prayer. The tactile sensation of playing with pebbles while reflecting on needs and desires helps clarify them and store them in somatic memory during prayer.

As I walked, I used Psalm 145:15-17 to guide my prayer: "The eyes of all look to you, and you give them their food in due season. You open your hand, satisfying the desire of every living thing. The Lord is just in all his ways and kind in all his doings." God provides for our needs *and* desires.

In kindness, God created us to thrive and experience the fruit of shalom—a sense of wholeness rooted in the soil of God's good purposes and restorative kingdom mission. What's important *for* me determines how to survive. What's important *to* me is what makes me come alive. Balancing these two desires is how I thrive.

Passing one stone at a time from my right to my left hand, I reflected on what is important *for* my survival, health, safety, and well-being, remembering that God sees my needs and promises to provide in due season. Then, I passed the stones from my left to my right hand while reflecting on what is important *to* me for living a meaningful life. Remembering that God satisfies the desires of every living thing, I can express my longings, values, and what brings joy.

By naming my needs and longings, I became aware of deeper, more authentic desires aligned with God's glorious kingdom (Ps 145:10-13). Our Spirit-infused desires draw us to peace, goodness, and the restoration work of shalom. They holistically encompass our physical, emotional, mental, and spiritual needs and longings. I concluded the walk with a deeper longing for the shalom, goodness, and restoration central to God's kingdom.

Praying with pebbles helps me hold my needs and longings more lightly as I wait for God to provide in due time. The smoothness of the pebbles calms my senses, while their firmness reminds me of God's enduring strength and kindness. This way of walking helps me discern what I need and want, advocate for myself and my daughter, and seek God's kingdom in the process.

WALK IT OUT

Scripture Meditation

Read Psalm 145:8-19. Focus phrase: *God satisfies my needs and longings.*

Walking Meditation

Before you go:

- Choose a path where you can gather pebbles. Alternatively, use prayer beads or other natural items like acorns or seashells.

As you walk:

- **Remember** God's compassion, justice, and kindness.
- **Important for me.** While passing pebbles from your dominant hand to your nondominant hand, name what you need for survival, health, safety, and well-being.
- **Important to me.** While passing pebbles from your nondominant hand to your dominant hand, name the longings, values, and joys that give your life dignity and animate your sense of purpose.
- **Seek God's kingdom.** How do your needs and desires align with the shalom of God's kingdom? Can you entrust them to God's care?

Rest and Reflect

After your walk, reflect on this question: *What deeper desires can I discern that help me seek God's kingdom?*

WALK 27

Birdwatching

Rewilding Faith

Great Spirit, Wild Goose of the Almighty,
be our eye in the dark places, be our flight
in the trapped places, be our host in the wild places,
be our brood in the barren places, be our
formation in the lost places.

RAY SIMPSON, *COMMON PRAYER*[1]

LIKE A CAGED BIRD, Mandy Smith felt trapped by the cultural expectations surrounding her church leadership role. While taking a walk to clear her mind, she noticed a flock of geese flying overhead. Mesmerized, Mandy observed that the geese did not plan to form a V-shape. Instead, "each goose attends to the art of sensing that slip-stream sweet spot," she explained in her book *Unfettered.* Geese instinctively fly in formation by paying attention to each other, rotating leadership, and finding the "space where the wind is kind." Stopped in her tracks, Mandy confessed to the wind: *I want to fly like that!* Learning to fly like a goose became her quest as she set out to practice a more childlike—and goose-like—faith.

A goose-like faith also inspired Celtic Christians, who adopted the wild goose as a symbol of the Holy Spirit. Captivated by God's beautiful and untamed movements, Irish pilgrims set out to *fly like that!* According to *The Anglo-Saxon Chronicle*, trusting entirely in God's guidance and provision, they cast their oars into the sea, declaring, "For the love of God, we want to be on pilgrimage but care not where."

For the love of God, the first disciples followed Jesus to God knows where. Following Christ is frustrating if we insist on knowing where we are going or sticking to a schedule. Jesus pointed to the birds as symbols of faith—a willingness to follow without an itinerary or promises of ease, safety, or comfort. Releasing preconceived ideas and controlled outcomes, faith trusts in God's daily provision and companionship. The pilgrimage to *God knows where* leads to our most authentic self—unattached to status, role, possessions, wealth, or power—which frees us to be guided by our values, virtues, and sense of calling. Pilgrims, like migrating birds, are guided by a deep *sensing of the slipstream sweet spot* that compels us to the heart of God.

Like Mandy, I love to birdwatch on my walks. Observing birds can stimulate a state of flow—the time-blurred experience of energized absorption in something meaningful beyond ourselves. Because birds can be elusive, birdwatchers learn to rely on less dominant senses, such as hearing and spatial awareness, to track them. Similarly, faith encourages us to follow by listening rather than seeing.

Faith isn't primarily a function of the intellect. Faith functions like the sensory system of the soul, relying on our less dominant senses to make sense of what we cannot explain. Faith is an orientation and movement toward God when we lack certainty about what lies ahead. Just as magnetic fields mysteriously guide birds during migration, faith compels us to pursue the Wild Goose without a map or itinerary, pointing our heart's compass toward God, the source and object of our faith.

In the journal *Ecopsychology*, Christoph Randler and colleagues state that birdwatching reduces stress, boosts well-being, and leads to "restoration, detachment, and experiencing freedom." I feel these benefits when I remove my earbuds and listen to the birdsong bidding me to release my need to control outcomes and embrace God's delight. For the love of God, I tune my senses to hear the Spirit's wild goose–like call to rewild my faith and follow without care. And when my faith wavers, I seek the slipstream's kind wind and recall Isaiah's promise: "Those who wait for the Lord shall renew their strength; they shall mount up with wings like eagles; they shall run and not be weary; they shall walk and not faint" (Is 40:31).

Tips for birdwatching: Go early in the morning when birds are active, and wear neutral colors to blend in. Bring binoculars, guidebooks, or the Merlin app. Take your time. Focus on your less dominant senses, staying curious about what God might reveal through birds.

WALK IT OUT

Scripture Meditation

Read Matthew 6:25-34. Focus phrase: *Learn faith from the birds.*

Walking Meditation

Before you go:

- Choose a path in a park, nature preserve, or wetland with birds. If you cannot find birds, listen to an audio recording of birdsong.

As you walk:

- **Slow down** and move quietly to avoid scaring the birds. Breathe deeply and detach from your cares.
- **Engage your senses,** noticing which ones you rely on most and exploring your less dominant senses. Reflect on your faith as a sensory experience.
- **Observe** the wildness of birds and what they teach you about rewilding your faith. Where are you too tame or caged to follow the Wild Goose? Where do you desire greater trust in God's guidance and provision?

Rest and Reflect

After your walk, reflect on this question: *Where is God calling me in a new direction or inviting me to rewild my faith?*

WALK 28

Walking Barefoot

Grounding in Hope

People usually consider walking on water or in thin air a miracle. But I think the real miracle is . . . to walk on earth.

THICH NHAT HANH, *THE MIRACLE OF MINDFULNESS*

STEPPING OFF THE MANICURED lawns of a retreat center, I hoped to find restoration for my weary soul in the wild Colorado foothills. I noticed hoofed, clawed, and pawed tracks in the dried earth, and my heart skipped as I thought about Colorado's wildlife: elk, hawk, mountain lion, bear. Examining the largest track, I found a heel, arch, and five toes—a human! Additional wildlife came to mind: rattlesnakes, spiders, and cacti! Why was a human walking barefoot on this wild landscape?

Following the tracks, I resisted an urge to take off my shoes. I love walking barefoot on sand and grass, but not the wilderness. An inner voice spoke: *You've lost connection with the good earth*. I kept walking, feeling a prickly awareness of my tendency to avoid pain. The voice persisted: *Stepping toward restoration and healing requires feeling weakness and vulnerability. Slow down and pay attention; I want to show you something.*

Reluctantly, I slipped off my shoes and nestled my toes in the dewy red earth. This wasn't the restoration path I had hoped for.

Grounding into the cold soil, I joined the parade of footprints. As grit collected between my toes, a painful memory stirred. With each step forward, my mind wandered back in time, wondering where Jesus was in the experience. I felt surprised to imagine him rubbing my feet—soothing my anxiety and pain. As my feet pressed into the earth, I felt the pressure of his hands on my feet. Each slow step relieved my pain and grounded me in hope: God with me.

Ancient people believed that healing begins at the feet. Pilgrims walked barefoot in solidarity with the suffering of Christ, the poor, and the land. Each step expressed an audacious hope for personal and collective healing. Recent studies confirm the link between barefoot walking and healing. According to a 2015 multidisciplinary study published by James Oschman and colleagues in the *Journal of Inflammation Research*, walking barefoot—also called earthing or grounding—connects the body's electrical system with the earth's natural electric charge, which boosts immune response, decreases inflammation and pain, and speeds wound healing.

As I returned to the manicured lawns of the retreat center, I passed a statue of Our Lady of Perpetual Help and gasped—baby Jesus had lost a sandal. The icon illuminated afresh the hopeful mystery of Christ's full humanity and divinity. According to tradition, Christ's sandaled foot is tied to earth's suffering, while his bare foot is unshackled from sin and death. The loosened sandal connects me to the earth's sufferings even as I totter toward a promised restoration.

Hope is painful and courageous. "Those who hope in Christ can no longer put up with reality as it is, but begin to suffer under it, to contradict it," writes Jürgen Moltmann in *Theology of Hope*. "The goad of the promised future stabs inexorably into the flesh of every unfulfilled present." Bound to the groaning earth, barefoot walking grounds us in the wild mystery: *Christ in you, the hope of glory* (Col 1:27).

Hope begins with the feet—grounded in a prickly awareness that we straddle earth and heaven. Hope does not passively wait for future restoration. Instead, hope actively seeks the greater good and the glory of God in each step bound to the groaning earth.

Begin this walk by removing your shoes and pressing your bare feet into the ground. Notice the sensations of temperature, textures, and pressure. Reflect on where you need hope, healing, or restoration. Feel the grit between your toes and ask: *Where is Jesus?* Allow barefoot Christ to loosen your sandals, wash your feet, and soothe your aches. Join the parade of barefoot pilgrims leaving their tracks in the mud to honor the earth, walk alongside the suffering, and seek a glimpse of the wholeness to come in this present life—starting with your feet.

Tips for barefoot walking: Begin slowly and carefully, walking on smooth or soft surfaces like grass, sand, or dirt. Stay alert for sharp objects, hot surfaces, and wildlife. Engage your senses to connect with the earth and remain open to divine revelations. If you have concerns, check with your doctor first and try standing, sitting, or lying on the ground instead of walking.

WALK IT OUT

Scripture Meditation

Read Psalm 33:16-22. Focus phrase: *I hope in God's steadfast love.*

Walking Meditation

Before you go:

- Choose a path where you can safely walk barefoot.

As you walk:

- **Go slowly** and feel the ground with your feet. Pay attention to the thoughts, memories, and emotions that arise.
- **Ground** your feet into the earth as you ground your hope in God's abiding love. Look for signs of life and renewal amid the grit and brokenness.
- **Hope**. What do you hope for? Notice how hope feels in your body. What does it feel like when hope is lacking?
- **Seek.** What steps can you take to pursue future wholeness in the unfulfilled present?

Rest and Reflect

After your walk, reflect on this question: *What courageous and transformative hope can I allow God's steadfast love to inspire?*

WALK 29

Labyrinth Dancing

Restorative Play

Might a hand reach out and lead us into the divine dance, *whispering in our ears that we were always made for this?*

WILLIAM PAUL YOUNG, FORWARD TO *THE DIVINE DANCE*

A	I	S	E	L	C	E	C	L	E	S	I	A
I	S	E	L	C	E	A	E	C	L	E	S	I
S	E	L	C	E	A	T	A	E	C	L	E	S
E	L	C	E	A	T	C	T	A	E	C	L	E
L	C	E	A	T	C	N	C	T	A	E	C	L
C	E	A	T	C	N	A	N	C	T	A	E	C
E	A	T	C	N	A	S	A	N	C	T	A	E
C	E	A	T	C	N	A	N	C	T	A	E	C
L	C	E	A	T	C	N	C	T	A	E	C	L
E	L	C	E	A	T	C	T	A	E	C	L	E
S	E	L	C	E	A	T	A	E	C	L	E	S
I	S	E	L	C	E	A	E	C	L	E	S	I
A	I	S	E	L	C	E	C	L	E	S	I	A

Palindrome at the center of a labyrinth in Reparatus Basilica, circa 324.

LABYRINTHS HAVE LONG REPRESENTED the wonder of human imagination, story, and play. In an epic Greco-Roman myth, Prince Theseus saved Athenian youth from the man-eating Minotaur imprisoned in a labyrinth. Unwinding a ball of golden thread behind him, Theseus navigated the winding pathway leading to the Minotaur. After slaying the beast, Theseus led the trapped souls to freedom by retracing the path marked with thread.

Early Christians adapted this myth to portray Christ's redemption from sin, defeat of the devil, and guidance to eternal life. The fourth-century Basilica of Saint Reparatus in North Africa featured an extraordinary mosaic labyrinth. Instead of a monster at the center, the golden thread led to a square-shaped word game in which the words *Sancta Ecclesia* ("Holy Church") could be read vertically and horizontally in hundreds of possible combinations.

During the Middle Ages, clergy in Auxerre, France, engaged in an exuberant Easter labyrinth dance, joyfully reenacting Christ's triumph and redemption. While the organ bellowed, clergy sang, tossed a ball, and shouted at the devil while dancing around the labyrinth. The Easter labyrinth dance was a liturgy of play, allowing clergy to set aside the heavy Lenten script and improvise their role in the narrative of Christ's victory. Play recharged their energy, refreshed their perspective, and restored their sense of self. In *Flourishing in Ministry,* University of Notre Dame professor Matt Bloom states that restorative play is essential for relieving stress and preventing burnout.

Play invites a restorative spirituality that draws us into the great redemptive dance. Suggesting that God takes play quite seriously, Thomas Merton wrote in *New Seeds of Contemplation*, "The Lord plays and diverts Himself in the garden of His creation, and if we could let go of our own obsession with what we think is the meaning of it all, we might be able to hear His call and follow Him in His mysterious, cosmic dance." When we feel trapped in a role, bound to a script, and burdened by responsibilities, play doesn't dismiss the importance of our obligations. Instead, it reminds us to hold our expectations loosely, expand our perspective, and cultivate openness to God's mysterious desires. Play allows us to unwind the golden thread and join the labyrinth dance.

There are no right or wrong ways to walk a labyrinth. Following the example of ancient Christians, try walking it as a liturgy of play. Allow the turns to help you unwind and relax as you release your burdens and anxieties to God. Join the labyrinth dance with joyful movements that draw you into the Easter story. If a labyrinth is inaccessible, feel free to walk anywhere enjoyable. You might bring a hacky sack, work on a crossword puzzle, or play fetch with your dog.

The labyrinth dance unfolds in four movements: Feel, unwind, play, and renew:

Feel. As you enter the labyrinth, engage your senses and tune into the sounds of the cosmic dance heard in the rustling wind, birdsong, and the rhythm of your footsteps.

Unwind. Reflecting on your life, is there a role or desire you take too seriously? Imaging it as a ball of thread, unwind it as you move through the labyrinth.

Play. Infuse your imaginary ball with play by tossing, kicking, or swinging it along the path. Allow yourself to be drawn into the Easter dance alongside clergy singing, dancing, and shouting at the devil. What role in the redemption story can you improvise in your daily life?

Renew. As you play, notice what fresh perspectives or desires energize you. Allow your desires to dance with God's desires as you play, improvise, and dance. Return to your daily life carrying the spirit of play within you. Consider writing a poem in response or searching for the words *Sancta Ecclesia* in the Saint Reparatus palindrome puzzle.

WALK IT OUT

Scripture Meditation

Read Jeremiah 31:11-14. Focus phrase: *Dance with joy.*

Walking Meditation

Before you go:

- Choose a labyrinth or an enjoyable path in a natural setting.

As you walk:

- **Feel** the rhythm of God's cosmic dance erupting around you as you engage your senses.
- **Unwind.** Choose a desire or role you take too seriously. Imaginatively unwind it like a ball of yarn as you walk.
- **Play.** Reflecting on the Easter labyrinth dance, join the celebration and play with your imaginary ball. Improvise a role in Christ's redemption story.
- **Renew.** Notice any fresh perspectives or desires that arise. Allow your desires to harmonize with God's in the cosmic dance.

Rest and Reflect

After your walk, reflect on this question: *How can I carry the spirit of play with me in daily life?*

PART 6

The Pilgrim's Way

Above all, trust the slow work of God. In everything,
we are naturally impatient to reach the end immediately. We
want to skip the in-between stages
and be on the way to something unknown *and* new.
Yet, the law of progress requires that
we pass through stages of instability,
which may take a long time. . . .
So, let your ideas mature gradually—allow them
to grow and form without force or hurry.
Only God can say what this new spirit shaping
within you will be. . . . Give our Lord the benefit
of believing his loving hand is leading you . . .
and accept the anxiety of feeling
in suspense and incomplete.

PIERRE TEILHARD DE CHARDIN, *GENÈSE D'UNE PENSÉE*,
TRANSLATED BY DEBORAH GREGORY

WALK 30

Rucking

What to Carry and Leave Behind

All the art of living lies in a fine mingling of letting go and holding on.

HAVELOCK ELLIS, *AFFIRMATIONS*

HEFTING MY DAUGHTER ALINA'S backpack over my shoulders, I walked beside her the half mile to the bus stop. Her bag felt heavy with the tools necessary for a successful school day—a laptop, books, binders, pencils, and a water bottle. When a neighbor congratulated my daughter on getting me to carry the bag, I replied, "It's okay, I'm rucking!"

Rucking is walking with a heavy backpack. While *The New York Times* and *GQ* hailed rucking as the trending workout of 2024, humans have been rucking since Paleolithic times. Bipedalism—the ability to walk with two feet—frees our arms to work, play, and meaningfully connect. It enabled hunters to spear prey, process the meat, and haul it back to the community. With free hands, gatherers could forage, cook, and build shelters while carrying their children on their backs. God designed the human body for endurance, bearing weight, and social connection.

Today, ruckers are inspired by the many health benefits. The combination of cardiovascular and weight-bearing exercise strengthens the heart, tones muscles, and prevents bone-density loss without the impact of running or weight training. The rhythmic joint compression provides proprioceptive input, which helps the body improve balance, regulate emotions, and lift mood. It is a no-cost exercise that is easily incorporated into daily activities like shopping, walking meetings, or walking to the bus stop.

While the benefits of rucking are compelling, they aren't why I carry Alina's backpack. I do it because I love her. She carries it all day. I can take it to the bus stop. As a neurodivergent young woman, my daughter holds the extra weight of ableism and sexism. And when she experiences sensory overload, she says it feels like her backpack shrinks to doll size, which significantly limits the resources she can carry and use.

Rucking offers an ironic grace: bearing weight activates proprioception to help regulate the nervous system and expand our mental backpack. Dr. Linnea Passaler, founder of Heal Your Nervous System, states on the company website that carrying heavy objects is "like whispering to your nervous system that you are robust, capable, and resilient, one active movement at a time."

Adjusting the straps on Alina's backpack, I asked her if it ever felt too heavy. "No," she replied, "I only carry the essentials—besides, some weight is good." By carrying her essentials, she builds strength and endurance. However, Alina noted that we don't all carry the same weight, nor can we see what others carry. Some weights, like emotional heaviness, tough decisions, and unfair expectations, are onerous to hold without help. Other burdens we are not meant to carry at all: regret, resentment, shame, perfectionism, excessive possessions, and even good things that divert us from our calling.

Reflecting on these unhealthy burdens, Alina said, "Maybe it's good that they feel heavy. The weight motivates us to deal with them—to ask forgiveness, get help, or make changes we want to avoid." Squeezing her hand, I emphasized the best feature of rucking: carrying weight on our backs frees our hands to reach out and care for others.

Rucking as a spiritual practice is easy to begin—all you need is a backpack and something to put inside it. A bag of rice or a few water bottles are simple to pack and can symbolize your essential needs. Consider adding items that represent the work or responsibilities you are called to carry. Start light, with 10–15 percent of your body weight, and gradually add more as you build strength, never exceeding one-third of your body weight. Walk your usual route, maintaining good posture by keeping your shoulders over your hips. If you decide to take rucking seriously, seek out proper gear, including a hip belt.

Rucking invites three spiritual wayfinding questions: *What essentials are mine to carry? What can I leave behind? What can I carry for someone else?* When you feel the extra weight, welcome every emotion that arises, trusting the heavy work your body is doing to help you regulate, grow strong, and build endurance. Allow God to whisper through your nervous system: *You are more robust, capable, and resilient* than you realize.

WALK IT OUT

Scripture Meditation

Read Exodus 12:31-39. Focus phrase: *Carry what you need.*

Walking Meditation

Before you go:

- Put weighted items in a backpack. Consider adding items that represent your work or responsibilities.
- Choose a path you walk regularly or enjoy.

As you walk:

- **Notice** how the extra weight feels on your back. What does carrying weight on your back free your hands to do?
- **Consider** the weight you carry in life. Which burdens feel the heaviest? How does it feel to carry that weight?
- **Examine** the three wayfinding questions:
  - *What essentials are mine to carry?*
  - *What can I leave behind?*
  - *What can I carry for others?*

Rest and Reflect

After your walk, reflect on this question: *What message of resilience and endurance do I need to hear and embrace?*

WALK 31

Japanese Interval Walking

Cultivating Inner Strength

Adopt the pace of nature.

RALPH WALDO EMERSON,
LECTURES AND BIOGRAPHICAL SKETCHES

FUMBLING OVER MY WORDS at the end of a difficult day, I told my daughter Alina, "You're stronger than you thonk." With a silly slip of the tongue, my tired brain awkwardly mashed the words *thought* and *think* into *thonk*. After a confused moment, we burst into cathartic laughter. That mistake became a beautiful reminder that it's okay to struggle, fail, and get tripped up. The laughter helped us recover a little strength. Tomorrow, we would rise to tackle new challenges with God's help.

Our family has since adopted the silly phrase *you're stronger than you thonk* as a reminder of God's help in the past and the help we will receive when facing future difficulties. More than physical brawn, true strength grows amid the intervals of work and recovery as we navigate life's challenges. Inner strength draws from the confidence of God's loving support to do more than we *thonk* possible.

Not far from my childhood home in Japan, people recovering from lifestyle-related diseases are also discovering that they are stronger than they *thonk.* Researchers at Matsumoto's Shinshu University developed a strength-training program called Interval Walking Training, or IWT. According to a 2024 episode of *Medical Frontiers* titled "New Findings in Walking and Running," lives are being transformed through the incredible benefits of interval walking: lowered blood pressure, enhanced metabolic function, stabilized glucose levels, and alleviated symptoms of depression, all while reducing medical expenses by an impressive 20 percent.

Japanese Interval Walking is a 3×3 protocol that alternates between three minutes of relaxed walking and three minutes of fast walking. Walkers gauge a relaxed pace by their ability to comfortably chat with a walking partner. During a fast pace, they find it difficult to talk or sing. If walkers can no longer smile, they are likely pushing themselves too hard.

Remarkably, walking for just thirty minutes a day at alternating speeds yields greater health benefits than walking 10,000 steps a day at a constant speed, according to a 2021 study by Dr. Kate Francis and her colleagues published in the *Journal of Sports Sciences.* In addition to health benefits, IWT enables walkers to connect with their bodies, build confidence, and rejuvenate their strength.

The first time I tried Japanese interval walking, I felt invigorated. The intervals encouraged me to extend beyond my comfortable pace and to embrace my need for rest and recovery. When Alina asked to join me on an interval walk, I asked what spiritual lessons she gleaned from the physical practice.

"There's an element of self-discovery," she replied. "You don't know what you can do until you try. God already knows what we are capable of, and with his help, we can do more than we imagine." Her words echo Paul's encouragement to the Ephesians, urging them to find rest in God's love and to allow Christ to strengthen them to do more than they could ask or imagine—more than they *thonk.*

Spiritual wayfinders can nurture both physical and spiritual strength through interval walking. Alternating between fast and slow paces for three to five cycles encourages healthy rhythms of work and rest. While walking slowly, we're reminded of God's care, provision, and the invitation to rest. Slowing down allows us to reflect on the obstacles, fears, and failures that hold us back in life. It's in these moments of gentle movement that we can talk, sing, and smile while reconnecting with God's sustaining love.

Speeding up, we ask God for the strength to face life's challenges and extend beyond our comfort zone. Reflecting on the areas of life where we are *all talk and no walk*, we seek God's empowerment to step forward. And if our smiles fade, each heavy breath prompts us to evaluate our tendency to push too hard or in unhealthy ways. Moving through the low-intensity and high-intensity intervals, we discover that *we're stronger than we thonk*, and with God's help, we can do more than we imagined.

WALK IT OUT

Scripture Meditation

Read Ephesians 3:16-20. Focus phrase: *With God's power, I can do more than I imagine.*

Walking Meditation

Before you go:

- Choose a path you enjoy walking.

As you walk:

- **Stretch** your arms as high and wide as you can reach. Imagine yourself within the breadth and depth of God's love.
- **Slow walk** for three minutes, allowing yourself to relax and connect with what is around you. Are there areas in life where you need to slow down and rest?
- **Fast walk** for three minutes, noticing changes in your breath, muscles, pulse, and voice. Are there areas where you can take on more challenges?
- **Alternate** slow and fast walking for three to five cycles.

Rest and Reflect

After your walk, reflect on this question: *What areas of my life can be strengthened through healthy intervals of work and rest?*

WALK 32

Rogation

Beating the Bounds

In every walk with Nature one receives far more than he seeks.

JOHN MUIR, *STEEP TRAILS*

I LIVE ON LAND WITH A HISTORY of violence and oppression. The Timucua people once thrived here until European diseases wiped out their communities. Plantation owners seized the land and beat the jungle into farmland using the forced labor of three hundred enslaved people. During the Second Seminole War, the plantation was burned as Seminoles protested their forced removal from their ancestral land.

The plantation ruins are now a state park. Reclaimed by the jungle, the land is healing, wildlife is finding refuge, and the ecosystem is growing stronger. People also enjoy restorative walks amid the lichen-covered trees, which cleanse the air. Society is slower to heal—violence, disease, and racism continue to plague our community. With this history in mind, I set out on a rogation walk through the park.

Rogation is a Latin word meaning "to ask." In the fifth century, Bishop Mamertus of Vienne, located in modern France, instituted rogation days in response to the violence of war and the devastation caused by earthquakes, drought, and fires that ravaged the people and the land. Mamertus rallied the people to an intercessory walk, seeking God's mercy in their time of need.

The tradition spread throughout Europe with grand processions of parishioners walking the boundary lines of their land or parish—a practice called *beating the bounds*. Asking for God's bounty, they scattered seeds, planted seedlings, and blessed the calloused hands of farmers along the way. Sometimes, priests sprinkled holy water on the land or turned a child upside down to bless a boundary marker with their head. Rogation intertwined joyful celebration with aching lament as the community sought God's protection and mercy upon the people and land.

While the church calendar designates four rogation days each year (April 25 and the three days leading up to the feast of Ascension), the practice of rogation is in decline. We have lost connection to the land and our neighbors. We shy from penitence and communal lament. But if we listen, the land and people continue to groan. A revival of rogation can begin by incorporating prayers of intercession, confession, and blessing into our daily walks.

Rogation moves in three parts: gratitude, groaning, and blessing:

Gratitude. Often walked in springtime, rogation celebrates new life and God's provision. Children memorized boundary lines by beating them with branches as adults sang litanies and drank ale. Today, families continue this tradition while walking the boundaries of homes, neighborhoods, schools, workplaces, or churches.

Groaning. Rogation includes prayers of sorrow, lament, and protection. It encourages us to listen to the land's groaning from natural disasters, pollution, and overdevelopment, and to pay attention to the struggles of our neighbors. By watering the earth, we commit to restorative action in the world.

Blessing. Blessing is a cry for life. As a pilgrimage of blessing, rogation actively seeks the good of others. Along the way, we celebrate signs of God's life-giving presence and beseech the author of life to restore the land and heal our lives. The celebratory procession inspires us to call forth life and participate in creation's renewal.

Using a water bottle and a fallen palm branch, I *beat the bounds* of the park near my home, splattering water on the earth, trees, and even a startled lizard. As I improvised a wandering liturgy of petition and blessing, I realized the land didn't need my blessing to heal. That's not how blessing works. Blessing acknowledges God's life and provision already at work. Where violence, disease, and oppression abound, blessing calls forth the restorative life of God. Blessing recognizes our interconnectedness with one another and the land, insisting that we all thrive.

My walk was a small, embodied attempt at rogation: Ask. Wave a branch. Give a blessing. Honor interdependence. Offer a drop of water wherever possible. I felt the joy of nature's renewal, yet my community still groans. Scattering water with a broken palm branch, I embraced a defiant hope. With openhanded trust, I asked God to restore and flourish the land and my community. Although rogation is a practice of asking, it asks something of us. Rogation asks us to orient our lives toward God's love and cultivate the life of the world.

WALK IT OUT

Scripture Meditation

Read Psalm 65:9-13. Focus phrase: *God cares for the land and makes it abundant.*

Walking Meditation

Before you go:

- Choose a path around your home, neighborhood, campus, workplace, church, or parish.
- Bring a bottle of water and a small branch. Consider inviting friends, family, or neighbors.

As you walk:

- **Gratitude.** Look for signs of life, renewal, and flourishing, and offer gratitude.
- **Groan.** Consider the history of the land. Acknowledge signs of oppression, pollution, or overdevelopment, and offer penitence and lament where you can.
- **Bless** as you spray water on the land and call forth God's abundant life. What steps can you take toward healing and restoration?

Rest and Reflect

After your walk, reflect on this question: *How can I tend to the flourishing of others? What needs to be tended in me?*

WALK 33

Walk Together

Uniting Steps, Awakening Joy

Whenever you go out, walk together,
and when you reach your destination, stay together.

THE RULE OF ST. AUGUSTINE

MY FAMILY ENJOYS WALKING together after dinner. However, our progress and pace slowed dramatically after my ankle injury. Taking my hand, my husband adjusted his long, purposeful stride to match my short, limping hobbles. Those slow recuperation walks were both humbling and tender as we learned and relearned how to cooperate while walking together.

Walking with others fosters social bonding. When two people walk in step, their bodies and brains synchronize subconsciously. It sounds beautiful, but moving in sync takes work. My injury highlighted how challenging it is for people with different builds and abilities to align their steps and speed. Yet, when matching our steps with another person, we synchronize heart rate, breath, and even brain activity. Ana Lucía Valencia and Tom Froese stated in the journal *Neuroscience of Consciousness* that the interbrain activity induced through synchronized movement may even extend consciousness between people.

Humans are designed for social walking. While my family enjoys walking together in our quiet neighborhood, we also have a knack for stumbling on political protests when we travel. The sound of drums, honk bands, and chanting draws us in. Collective movements, like peaceful protest marching and pilgrimage, lead to what anthropologist Emile Durkheim called a *collective effervescence*—a joyful sense of solidarity that emerges from participating in something beyond ourselves. According to research led by Miiamaaria Saarela and published in *Social Neuroscience*, even the sound of two or more footsteps activates the brain for social interaction and identity formation. Walking together fosters an embodied cognition that helps people bond and coalesce around shared values and goals.

Walking in sync requires patience and care. "We are naturally impatient to reach the end immediately," wrote Jesuit priest Pierre Teilhard de Chardin in a letter to his cousin. It's easy for us to leave others behind in our rush forward. However, falling out of step can stir up agitation, distrust, and discord.

The human body is not only designed to walk with others, but also to walk with God. The theme of walking with God ambles through Scripture. God walked with Adam and Eve in the Garden, walked with Enoch, and walked with Noah. God walked with the Israelites for forty years in the wilderness. The disciples walked with Jesus, and the apostles walked with the Spirit, who continues to guide us. God doesn't lead with urgency toward a destination. God meets us where we are.

Walking with God looks different for each person and stage of life. It looks like Abraham's faith in leaving family and country for an unknown land. It looks like Ruth's devotion to Naomi in living as a refugee. It's the compassion of the Good Samaritan who slows down to care for a stranger. It's Elisha's faithful companionship to Elijah, David's dancing with servants, Jonah's solemn, obedient march to Ninevah, and the Israelite's joyful cadence during festival pilgrimages. As the disciples walked with Jesus, they learned the rhythms of God's kingdom—a cadence we are invited to join as we walk with God in our daily lives.

My favorite example of God walking with us is the parable of the prodigal son, who left home to squander his inheritance and later returned in humiliation. When the father saw the son a long way off, he ran to him. Together, they walked the long path back home. As you walk, imagine the father and son strolling, arm in arm. Consider the gifts of shoes and robes the father gives the son, which signify protection and belonging. Walking together, the bond of love strengthened, identity restored, and a grand celebration of *collective effervescence* marked the son's return.

While walking with a partner, in a group, or alone in an area where others are walking, notice how it feels to walk with others. Pay attention to the words, gestures, or postures used in navigating a shared space, observing the ease or difficulty of walking together. Contemplate your walk with God, acknowledging where you feel synchronized or out of step. Do you impatiently push ahead or distractedly lag behind? Finally, imagine you are the prodigal son walking alongside his father. What does God say to you? What gifts does God offer you for the journey? Reflect on how the long, slow walk with God shapes your identity and inspires you to walk more purposefully with others.

WALK IT OUT

Scripture Meditation

Read Luke 15:11-24. Focus phrase: *God walks with me.*

Walking Meditation

Before you go:

- Choose a path where others may be walking, like a busy park, urban area, college campus, or shopping mall. Walk with a partner, group, or alone.

As you walk:

- **Notice** how your movements synchronize with others. How does it feel to walk in sync with others? How does it feel to fall out of step?
- **Synchronize** your walk with God. Where do you feel in sync or out of step?
- **Receive.** Imagine you are the prodigal son walking home with the father. What does the father say or give to you?

Rest and Reflect

After your walk, reflect on this question: *How can I walk more meaningfully with God and with others?*

May the road rise up to meet you.
May the wind be always at your back.
May the sun shine warm upon your face;
the rains fall soft upon your fields and until we meet again,
may God hold you in the palm of His hand.

IRISH BENEDICTION

Acknowledgments

I AM GRATEFUL TO SHARE THIS JOURNEY with many incredible companions. Thank you to Bob Fryling for encouraging me to step forward with the seed of an idea. To Christianne Squires, my talented book midwife, thank you for skillfully helping me nurture it to life. My deepest gratitude extends to the fantastic InterVarsity Press team—especially Cindy Bunch, Kelli Trujillo, and Lori Neff—who expertly helped shape and share this book. I could not have reached this milestone without my fellow pilgrims who lent their sacred stories, delightful insights, and steady support—especially Marissa Lapish, Alexai Perez, Kayla Roberts, Kathy Robinson, Joan Grennan, Hillary Walker, Kim Koi, Tara Owens, Stacy Balfour, Matt Tebbe, Mandy Smith, and Cody Wood. To Ben Trube, I extend recursive thanks for the lesson on fractals. I deeply appreciate Ray Simson for kindly permitting the use of his "Wild Goose" prayer, Andrea Sarubbi at The Pope's Video for generously sharing their "Prayer for Formation in Discernment," and Mary Eggleston at Jesuit Archives & Research Center for helping me track down an elusive quote by Fr. Whelan, SJ. Finally, heartfelt thanks to my family for being open to exploring new—and sometimes unconventional—ways of walking together.

Notes

PART 2: EXPLORING YOUR EMOTIONS

[1]Joseph Whelan, SJ, Talk to the Communities, Maryland Province, 1981-82: "On Apostolic Freedom, Mobility, Community, and on the Province, National, International Context of our Jesuit Mission."

PART 5: EXERCISING DISCERNMENT

[1]"Prayer for Formation in Discernment," Pope's Worldwide Prayer Network, from The Pope Video, July 2025, read by Pope Leo XIV. Used by permission.

WALK 27: BIRDWATCHING: REWILDING FAITH

[1]Ray Simpson, "Great Spirit, Wild Goose," from *A Holy Island Prayer Book: Prayers and Readings from Lindesfarne* (Church Publishing Inc., 2002). Used by permission.